# The Making of the Wight

### By

### J.C. Medland

*St Thomas's Square Newport in the early nineteenth century.*
*Courtesy of Isle of Wight County Records Office.*

# The Making of the Wight

By

J.C. Medland MSc

Published by The Isle of Wight Beacon Ltd

Published by
The Isle of Wight Beacon Ltd.
25 Daish Way
Newport
Isle of Wight PO30 5XJ

ISBN No 978-1-904-14910-3

Cover design by Katerina Przygonski
Typesetting and artwork by Matthew Power

Printed by the West Island Group Ltd
Afton Road, Freshwater,
Isle of Wight PO40 9TT

# Contents

# Acknowledgements

I would like to acknowledge the assistance of the I.W. County Records Office, I.W. Archaeological Service, Hampshire & I.W. Trust for Maritime Archaeology, Carisbrooke Castle Museum, Dimbola Lodge Museum, Dr Robin McInnes OBE, Portsmouth City Museum, East Cowes Heritage Centre, Ordnance Survey, I.W. Steam Railway, Brading and Newport Villas, National Trust, English Heritage, Shanklin Chine Heritage Centre, The Royal Yacht Squadron, The I.W. Library Service and all those who have contributed to the writing and illustration of this book:

I would also like to thank my family for all their help in the production of this book.

# Introduction

There are times when we must all wonder about the past generations and the way they saw the world, and how they contributed to make the world as we see it now. As so much of the present landscape seems to be consumed by modern development it is perhaps even more important that we preserve a vision of our past before it is irredeemably lost.

The history of the Isle of Wight is a unique history fashioned by a particular geography, geology, climate, as well as the unexpected individual turns and stumbles of human history. At the same time it provides an insight into a wider history. It acts as a microcosm of the history of England, of Britain, of Europe and the wider world.

The stories that make up this book were originally published as monthly "Island Story" articles in the Isle of Wight Beacon magazines starting in January 2005. Such was the interest that these stories have generated among our readers that we have decided to serialise them in an annual sequence of books as the stories continue to be published.

They provide a welcome opportunity to revisit some of the most important moments in our Island story, the terrors and triumphs of foreign invasion, our inventions and achievements, forgotten battles in foreign lands, heroic deeds in shipwreck dramas, our unique feudal dynasty of Norman lords, our ongoing relationship with the kings and queens of Wessex, England and Britain and our place in the evolution of British and global art and science.

These are just some of the subjects that come to life when one investigates the history of our Island. Some of the stories take the form of rediscoveries, as we uncover the genius of the greatest Islander of all, Robert Hooke, whose reputation was carefully buried by Sir Isaac Newton three centuries ago, or the forgotten heroes of the First World War, disgraced by their general's surrender in Iraq, and the extraordinary tale of the Isle of Wight based space rocket programme. Other stories are well known, the incarceration of King Charles I in Carisbrooke, Queen Victoria's splendour at Osborne, Marconi's triumph with radio at the Needles, but often there is a lesser known twist in the tale.

In the absence of much previous historical research much of our history is preserved in myth and legends, each with some element of truth, like the Pied Piper of Newtown, possibly the precursor of the Piper of Hamelin, which recalls the arrival of the Black Death and reminds us of the political corruption of our once proud medieval boroughs. The Island today remains rich in historical records, to be found in ancient trackways and hedges as well as weathered parchment and faded tombstones. There is a great deal more to discover. I hope this book will be a stimulus to all of us who have an interest in the past to find out a little more, to discover more of this unique Island story, which casts a light on the wider history of our modern world.

I apologise to those of you who find it odd that the Island is referred to with a capital I and the Mainland with a capital M. This is a long-standing local tradition which somehow makes sense once you have lived here for some time.

# THE MAKING OF THE ISLAND

The creation of the Isle of Wight, when the Solent landscape finally flooded, is currently assumed to have occurred around 8,000 years ago, about the same time as the island of Britain finally separated from the continent of Europe. The direct cause of the flooding of the North Sea, English Channel and the Solent Valley by the ocean was the end of the last phase of the Ice Age, which occurred about 12,000 years ago. As the weight of the ice sheets over northern Britain melted the land began to rise, and is still rising, depressing glacier–free southern Britain into the rising seas which were filling with ice-meltwaters. This is a process that is still continuing, reminding us that the Island is a key test case for ongoing geographical forces that are shaping the modern world.

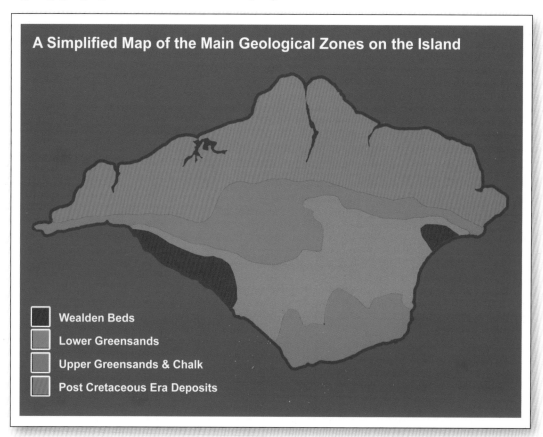

A Simplified Map of the Main Geological Zones on the Island

- Wealden Beds
- Lower Greensands
- Upper Greensands & Chalk
- Post Cretaceous Era Deposits

However the full explanation of how the flooding made our Island lies in its geological formation which takes us back to the time when dinosaurs roamed the Earth. The oldest surface strata on the Island are the Wealden Beds which are about 140 million years old. The Wealden beds at the north of Sandown Bay and around Brook Bay recall a time when this land was covered by shallow lagoons and they contain the Island's extraordinary treasure trove of dinosaur remains which makes the Island one of the top sites in the world for the discovery of new dinosaur material. At Hanover Point the remains of a fossil log jam can be seen at low tide. The early trees have petrified into a forest of lignite.

In the later part of the Cretaceous period (120-70 million years ago) the green sands and gaults of the southern central lowlands of the Wight were laid down providing some of our most fertile farmland. Then, over another immense period of about 50 million years, the surface area of the Island appears to have sunk to the bottom of a deep ocean. Huge deposits of chalk were laid down at a rate of about 1 centimetre every 1,000 years. The chalk represents the piled skeletons of tiny sea creatures which now form the larger skeleton of the Island and South East England.

Around 22 million years ago the African and European continental plates collided. Enormous tectonic pressures caused the deep layers of flat deposits to buckle. The spectacular result was the formation of the Alps. The shock-wave ripples of this gigantic event reached out to the substrata of what would be the Island. It created a wave of rock that raised the old Cretaceous strata to make the centre and south of the modern Island while bucking down below the modern sea level of what is now the English Channel and Solent and New Forest or "Hampshire Basin" before re-emerging as the South Downs. The mountains of the Wight might then have been some 600 metres high but tens of millions of years of erosion have worn them down to 230m.

Compared to the old Cretaceous rocks of the chalk "backbone" and uplifted southern strata, the clay and limestone of the northern half of the Island belongs to the more recent geological eras, deposited between 70 and 30 million years ago. Of particular importance to the Island was the Bembridge limestone which was created in a freshwater environment. It forms part of the natural sea wall of the northern and eastern coasts of the Wight. The final deposits on the Island were made in the last two million years, during wet phases of the "Ice Age" and include the fossils of early mammals.

The Island's range of geological material not only provides our unique fossil record but also explains the Island's geography, which in turn dictates our historic development. The Island is split into a series of different landscapes each attracting different plants and creatures, giving the Island an extraordinary range of biodiversity for its area.

Over the years underlying geography, combined with the climate has created distinctive patterns of human settlement. For example the clay and gravel northern lowlands where most Islanders now live was an uncultivated mostly woodland heath for much of our history. The earliest area of settled farming was the central ridge of chalk that rises out of the earth between the Needles in the west and Culver Cliff in the east. The east–west chalk upland provided a route for communication to complement to the north-south tidal estuaries. Most Roman villa sites are in this zone, and the main Saxon settlements at Carisbrooke and Calbourne.

There is a patchwork of agricultural settlement zones south of the downs on the more fertile green sands which have been settled and farmed since the Iron Age. The Southern chalk uplands were cleared at the same time as the central ridge with farming communities developing on the lower slopes. South of the uplands the Undercliff became detached by landslides over the last 10,000 years and was settled by Prehistoric peoples exploiting the coast for seafood.

# THE FIRST ISLANDERS

The first Islanders strictly speaking were those stone age humans who found themselves on the southern side of the new Solent sea around 8,000 years ago when the gyrating tides finally cut deep enough channels to flow from one end to out the other. However there were humans living on the land that would become the Island for thousands of years before. They had come to the warming sub-arctic tundra about 12,000 years ago to hunt herds of woolly mammoth after the end of the last Ice Age. These were nomadic peoples who followed the migrations of herds of wild animals the breeding cycles of marine organisms and the seasons of fruits and edible roots. They used and made stone tools to kill and process their daily needs, dressed in the skins of the animals they killed.

Their descendents found themselves in a changing, warming, environment. The tundra turned to brush and the brush grew into dark forest. With all the large animals killed these Stone Age Islanders would have had to rely more on seafood and fishing. There are 235 records from the "New Stone Age" period on the Island, about 10,000BC to 3,500BC. 77 are polished axes. Pottery remains have been found at four sites. There are long barrows and a mortuary enclosure for the dead, and various structures discovered off the submerged coast of Wootton. The finds indicate human settlement and activity was concentrated on the river valleys and coastal estuaries where marine food was plentiful.

## The Neolithic Revolution

By the time the first Stone Age peoples wandered our cold sub-arctic landscape, about 12,000 years ago, human history was beginning to undergo what is termed the "Neolithic Revolution". In various places around the world different communities were experimenting with domesticating captured wild animals and altering the condition and environments of the wild plants that they most commonly used. The nearest place this was happening was in the then fertile lands of south-west Asia. By 7,000BC this revolutionary technology had reached Egypt and by 5,000BC the Iraqis had developed all the basic techniques of modern agriculture, which slowly spread to and across Europe.

This first agricultural revolution reached Britain in about 4,500BC. At first the agricultural techniques were added to those of hunter-gathering, as a field might be cleared with fire to plant a crop and then abandoned again. This "slash and burn" agriculture continued the nomadic lifestyle of the Stone Age humans. However once people began to adopt settled agriculture, human society began to change fundamentally.

Settled agricultural communities began to grow in population. The annual surplus of harvests needed to be stored and protected. Some spare hands turned to crafts such as pottery and carpentry. Others specialised in warfare and religion. Surplus production meant more barter and trade between different settlements. It meant keeping records, which led to the invention of writing.

Individual families became particularly attached to the land they worked, developing the notion of private landed property. Over the centuries more complex social hierarchies developed into larger units from family to tribe, clan to kingdom. Marriage, slavery, inheritance and status became fixed by ceremony and custom.

## The Bronze Age

From 3,000BC down to about 1,600BC a complex British society was engaged in the extraordinary construction of the religious landscape of Stonehenge. By 2,000BC sea going clinker planked sailing and rowing ships were being built around Britain and were engaging in overseas trade. The Bronze/Iron Age (from about 2,150BC) marks another stage of human development. The ability to fashion metal tools gave people a far better range of tools and weapons. They buried their dead in sheltered chalk valleys. 200 burial mounds are recorded in the Island's upper landscape. The chalk downland was increasingly cleared for agriculture but the coasts, including the Undercliff remained important areas of settlement and exploitation. Iron Age hill forts have been identified at Yaverland and Chillerton. The excavation of Yaverland Fort in 2001 revealed it to be a triple ditch defensive system complete with walls and round-houses, and lots of pottery and domestic waste. The Chillerton site is a supposed unfinished promontory fort. It has a 275 foot rampart, 10 feet high and 60-70 feet wide.

## The Iron Age

The Iron Age (from about 750BC) combined with the coming of Celtic culture, originally from south eastern and central Europe. The peoples of Britain began to speak Celtic languages and developed large political units, kingdoms. The Island lay at a key position for both Atlantic and Central European trade routes. As the Romans conquered Gaul in the century before Christ, the Belgae peoples migrated into south east Britain bringing a more advanced culture and the first towns began to develop. The tribes of the south of England were starting to copy the Roman ways, even circulating their own coin. The importance of trade is attested by the fact that so many coins were minted on the Island from imported gold and silver. Fragments of pottery also show that the Island was importing wine. It seems clear that the economy of the Island was well integrated with the growing cross Channel trade with the Roman Empire in Gaul. There was a great deal of continuity between the Bronze-Iron Age Wight and Roman Vectis.

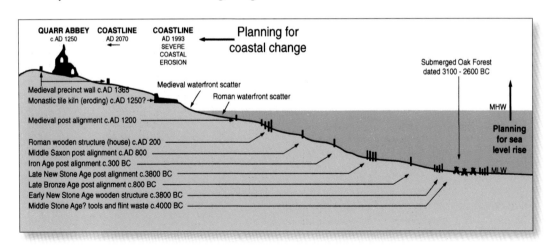

*This cross section of the submerging coastline produced by archaeologist David Tomalin and the I.W.Centre for the Coastal Environment gives us an insight into our past and a warning about our future.*
*To the far right the sea bed was still above the coastline some 5,000 years ago. Over the past 12,000 years sea levels around the Island have been rising following the last Ice Age which is also causing the landmass of Southern England to sink. This is because of the removal of the weight of ice from Northern Britain.*

*As the sea level has risen historic landscapes from the Stone Age onwards have been drowned and preserved in the marine silt. The archaeological research along the coast from Wootton to Seaview is bringing to light many prehistoric, Roman and Medieval marine structures. As we look to the future, we can see that our current coastline is under significant long term threat, particularly with accelerating sea level rises due to global warming.*

# IN ROMAN VECTIS AD43 – 410

*The interior of Newport Villa brought to life by members of the I.W. Council Heritage Service. Courtesy of the I.W. Museums Service.*

For almost four hundred years, the longest continuous period in our known political history, the Isle of Wight was ruled as an integral part of the Roman Empire. This was a period of prosperity and high culture that would not be reached again for over a thousand years.

The Roman Empire combined all the traditions of the Greek and the older near eastern civilisations with a Mediterranean-wide commercial system under the political mastery of a single metropolis. The British exported corn, cattle, gold, silver, iron, animal hides, slaves and hunting dogs in return for the many luxury goods of the empire, principally wine.

By the time the legions crunched ashore on Kent's beaches in AD42 the Islanders probably welcomed them compared to other Britons who never accepted conquest. The Island's Celtic farms, quarries and pottery kilns which were already exporting to the mainland continued and developed in the more stable politics that came with the empire. The empire also brought taxes. Taxes stimulated productivity and a market economy based on a stable currency. The imperial army and navy had huge needs for Island corn, meat and leather and the conquered British tribes each built new city capitols creating additional demand for the Island's Bembridge limestone quarries and Vectis ware kilns. Enterprising Islanders could now take advantage of the market to produce more and make profits to buy the vast range of luxury products that were now on offer.

The distinctive form of Roman settlement on Vectis, as the Romans named the Island, was the villa. A villa can be defined as a Romanised rural settlement, generally practising mixed farming, food processing and perhaps some manufacturing. The sites of up to eight Roman villas have been discovered on the Island so far. They are at Brading, Combley (Arreton), Newport, Carisbrooke, Clatterford, Bowcombe possibly, Rock (Brighstone) and Gurnard. They represent all the basic villa types of all the 700 villas found in the UK. Gurnard has already disappeared. It was discovered in the 1860s fifteen feet up in the crumbling cliff face and was rapidly excavated before it vanished into the sea. The location is unlike any other Island villa and it is speculated that it may have been a centre for the export of Bembridge limestone. In 70AD Island limestone was used in the construction of the palace of Fishbourne in Sussex.

The other seven villas all lie on the Island's central upland spine where the Celtic farmers were already settled. This position allowed the maximum possible exploitation of the Island's rich natural resources. Another advantage was that all the villas were linked by the ancient east-west road across the top of the downs. Of the other villas Carisbrooke was excavated crudely in 1859 and left open to the elements so that little can be learned. Clatterford lies just under the topsoil nearby. The site was bought by the IW Council to protect it from ploughing. It has never been excavated. Remains at Bowcombe have been found but the villa's status is unconfirmed. The best archaeological evidence comes from Newport, Combley, Rock and Brading.

# Daily life at the height of the Empire

In the first decades of Roman rule the Celtic Brading, Newport and Combley settlements are known to have transformed into quadrangular Roman buildings and would continue to develop and rebuild in Roman style for the next three centuries. At the peak of prosperity, about 250 - 300AD Vectis was a well populated rural Romano-Celtic-British society. The archaeological record tells us that the people of these villas lived to a high standard of living. In addition to farmers there were skilled craftsmen living on the Island as well as traders and mariners.

The villa dwellers practised advanced mixed farming with crop rotation and introduced rape, vetch and turnips to enrich the soil, as well as manure from the increasing herds of livestock. To the vegetable beds and orchard groves beside the villas they introduced carrots, celery, pears and plums. There were also new herbs; mint, parsley, rosemary, sage and thyme. Bee hives supplied honey and there were salt pans at Wootton and Yaverland.

The main cereal crops were wheat and barley which were grown on the chalk downs and fertile greensands south of the central downs. They were harvested with sickles and ground to flour with circular mill stones to be used for bread, beer, cake and pastries. Dairy and beef cattle grazed in the wet meadows where hay could also be harvested for winter feed with the newly introduced scythe. Chicken, geese, goats and oxen were raised. Horses were kept for hunting and donkeys used for transport. The chalk downs were used for sheep grazing and small fields for cultivation which can still be made out on aerial photos. The sheep wool was woven into cloth on simple looms. The wilderness was also harvested. The great northern forest was used for foraging pigs and for hunting deer, wild boar, storks, cranes and swans. The sea provided another rich source of protein, including vast numbers of oysters as well as the varied fisheries of Island waters.

These well-fed people did not dress as we think in a Roman way. Togas were formal dress for special occasions. In our climate they wore sensible wool and linen tunics and shirts, with trousers and leather boots for working outside. A British fashion export was a long, hooded woollen coat. Women had colourful shawls and wraps clasped with brooches complemented by bracelets, earrings, necklaces and decorated shoes.

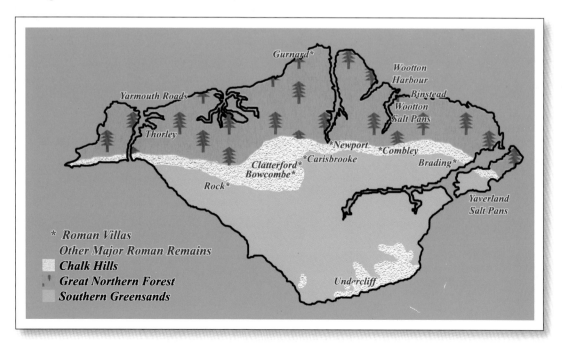

* Roman Villas
  Other Major Roman Remains
  Chalk Hills
  Great Northern Forest
  Southern Greensands

The villa homes looked very modern, with rectangular rooms furnished with chairs, couches, tables, wardrobes and shelves. The floors were sometimes underheated and decorated with stone mosaic and the walls beautifully painted. There were windows about a metre square, with shutters, grills and glass.

The walls were a metre high in stone, then timber framed, in filled with wattle and daub and plastered over. The roofs were hung with Vectis tiles or slabs of Bembridge limestone held with iron nails and lime mortar cement. Brading even had a front door lock and key and a circular stone pond in the garden.

*This cross section of the wall at Newport Villa shows both the modern look of the straight walls and square windows and the materials used in construction.*
*Courtesy of the Isle of Wight Museums Service.*

Three of the excavated villas, Brading, Newport and Combley had Roman baths and the Roman habits of cleanliness make their culture historically distinct. Along with the baths are a wide range of cosmetics. Although these were the foibles of the rich even the poorest Islanders living in their circular mud and thatch huts must have benefited from the peace and material prosperity of life in Roman Vectis. Much of the success of the agricultural economy relied on the easy access to markets. The Second Century geographer Ptolemy called the network of Solent waters the "Magnus Portus" of local and international trade. There is clear evidence of an anchorage off Yarmouth and at Wootton Creek.

Brading villa was directly linked to the Island's great eastern anchorage. South on the Undercliff a Celtic population continued into Roman times probably using fishing and collecting seafood as much as agriculture for a living. 1984 excavations near Yarmouth discovered Second and Third Century artefacts in the ploughsoil. Is this a maritime settlement perhaps exploiting the underlying outcrop of Bembridge limestone? Other significant finds were made at Binstead, another potential quarry site and literally thousands of Roman coins have been found in all parts of the Island.

These "Vectensians" lived in a truly multicultural society. Although the bulk of the population remained Celtic-British people came from every part of the empire and intermarried and exchanged ideas. There was now a bewildering variety of Gods from Celtic to Persian, Egyptian to Greek, one of which finally became official. In 313AD the Emperor Constantine made Christianity the imperial state religion.

*An artists impression of Combley Villa, Arreton.*
*Courtesy of the I.W. Museums Service.*

*One of the exquisite mosaics from Brading Villa which has been re housed
in an award winning museum. Courtesy of Brading Villa.*

## The decline and fall of Roman Vectis

By this time the Roman Empire was in economic and political decline. Emperor Constantine moved the imperial capital east from Rome to what is now Istanbul but would continue to be called Constantinople until it fell finally to the Turks in 1453. The empire in the west expired far more quickly. In the fourth century, 300-400AD, Vectis ware pottery seems to have fallen rapidly in production. In 367AD Roman Britain was attacked by Barbarians from all sides. The villas ceased to be luxurious as the rich owners seem to have fled, rather becoming working buildings.

At Brading for example the baths became an industrial building. Animals were butchered and ploughs stored on the beautiful mosaics. Part of the mosaic was destroyed to build a seed drier. Some kind of life continued to at least the reign of the last western Roman Emperor Honorious, 395-424. In the first decade of the fifth century, 400-410 the mainland provinces of the western Empire were overrun by invading German tribes. Britain fought on alone but the money economy and army had gone. Civilisation seems to have rapidly collapsed. This is reflected in the rapid disintegration of the remaining dilapidated buildings. They became quickly overgrown and often seem to have been completely forgotten. The best places now to get a feel for Roman Vectis are the villas of Brading and Newport, between them representing 10% of all preserved Roman villas open to the public in the country.

# THE ANGLO SAXON WIGHT
## AD400-1066

In the year 686 the prows of invading longships crunched on the Island's shore and disgorged a splashing army of helmeted Saxon warriors carrying spears, axes, bows and shields. They were led by a warrior chief of the epic-heroic school, a warlord-prince on a mission from God. King Caedwalla of Wessex was leading this, the last great Saxon invasion of the Island.

It was the end of the independent Jutish Kingdom of the Wight that seems to have existed for about 250 years. The story of their original invasions are lost to history but from the mid Fifth Century they ruled a pagan kingdom until Caedwalla's Christian victory. For all but 30 of the next 380 years to 1066, the Isle of Wight owed allegiance to the House of Wessex, the royal family from which our current monarchy takes its historic authority.

The House of Wessex, based at Winchester, was not only the longest reigning English royal dynasty, it was also the most important. During these violent "Dark Ages" the Christian Kingdom of England was fashioned out of tribal chaos.

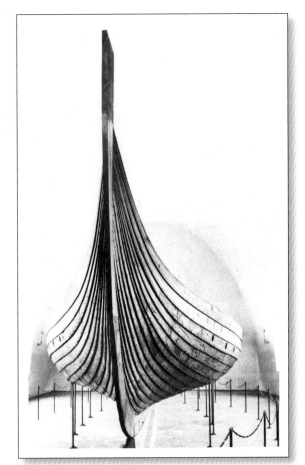

*This Gokstad Longship in Oslo gives an example of the ship design that enabled the English and later Viking invasions of the British Isles between the Fourth and Eleventh Centuries. Courtesy of the Gokstad Museum.*

*A map of former Roman Britannia in about 600 AD showing the seven principle English Kingdoms that had developed in the British Lowlands*

- - - - = **Roman Boundary**

**Northumbria**

**Mercia**

**East Anglia**

**Essex**

**Wessex**

**Kent**

**Sussex**

# The English Invasion of Vectis

The making of England began with the invasion of the former Roman province of Britannia by German-Danish tribes, principally the Angles, Jutes and Saxons in the Fifth Century. Originally employed as mercenaries to replace the departed Roman army, two Jutish warlords, defeated the British "tyrant" and in 456 established their own kingdom of Kent. Others soon followed their example.

Given its exposed position Vectis was probably one of the first territories to be ravaged and conquered. Following the sudden collapse of the Roman Empire the Vectensian population was trying to adapt to political anarchy as their society suddenly regressed into the Iron Age. This "Dark Age" is symbolized in archaeology by a dearth of British finds after 400AD. Society regressed to the point that people stopped using pottery.

The invaders were far better adapted to the subsistence economy and growing wilderness of the Island. By the end of the century a thriving successful population of Saxons and Jutes were burying their dead in spectacular cemeteries on Chessel and Bowcombe downs. The dead were accompanied by beautiful, highly crafted personal possessions. These invaders clearly had a rich culture with extensive European trade links. They were clearly the masters of the Island.

*Drawings of some of the Jutish grave goods excavated on Chessel Down in the Nineteenth Century. They are now kept in the British Museum. Courtesy of the Archaeological Service.*

One great question of history is what happened to the Celtic speaking, Christian, British population? It has long been assumed that they were killed off or fled. Many did indeed die in war and of hunger and disease. Others retreated west, to Cornwall and Wales, or sailed south-west, to colonise Amorica, now Brittany. However many more probably remained as slaves of the new English masters. It was in the interest of the invaders to keep the agricultural workforce who understood the land and how to exploit it. National DNA surveys suggest most of us are mostly descended from Stone Age Iberian stock with some Neolithic Middle Eastern genes with only about 15% of our genes from North-West Europe.

# The Jutish Kingdom of the Wight

In 530AD, according to Anglo-Saxon folk-lore later written down by the monk Bede, the Island was invaded and conquered by Cerdic, king of the West Saxons. The decisive battle was at Carisbrooke. In 534 he passed the Island to his Jutish nephews Stuf and Whitgar. Whitgar became the first Jutish monarch of this new dynasty that would rule this Island kingdom for one and a half centuries. He made his capital at Carisbrooke, and was buried there in 544.

By about 600AD, 150 years later, in what had been the lowlands of Christian Britannia seven principle pagan English kingdoms had emerged; Jutish Kent, the Angle territories of the Northumbrians, Mercians and East Anglians, and the eastern, southern and western Saxons of Essex, Sussex and Wessex.

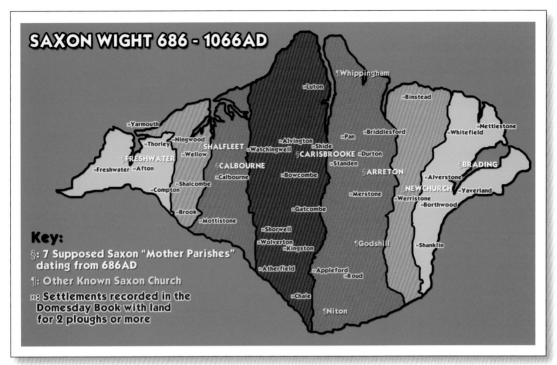

*A Saxon Parish Map showing significant farming.*

The Wight was a quasi independent kingdom as neighbouring Wessex conquered the south-west of Britannia. Place name evidence suggests the Jutish/Saxon populations settled the land around the northern rivers and the fertile south west. Mainland archaeology suggests they lived in scattered hamlets of a few families, fenced against wild animals. The main building was the hall, built with oak planks coated in twigs and clay. Each community was largely self-sufficient. The corn was ground on imported millstones. The wool was spun and woven on upright looms. Crude pottery was half baked in the open fire and simple metal working tasks attempted. Their pagan world was filled with gods and goddesses, spirits and ogres. They practiced astrology and witchcraft. Sacred ceremonies, including animal sacrifice, were performed at springs and streams, boundaries, trees and stones. At the Festival of the Birth of the Sun, which we now celebrate as Christmas, they dressed and danced in the skins and skulls of stags and cows.

While still engaged in their bitter war against the British, the Anglo-Saxon kingdoms were also fighting among themselves. After defeat by Wessex, the King of Kent welcomed the Roman Catholic Church in 595. The church provided literate, educated clerical administrators, who increased the power of the state. For a while Kent dominated the others so that by 650 all the other kings had adopted Christianity and each had their own bishop and clergy. As the seven kingdoms jostled for power the Island was increasingly a victim. Wessex invaded in 625. In 661 Wulfhere King of Mercia invaded and "laid waste to Wight". The climax came in the mid 680's when Caedwalla, King of Wessex set about the final conquest and Christianisation of southern England.

Not yet 30 Caedwalla had spent much of his life as a banished exile in the forest, but in one year he had taken the family throne, crushed Sussex, Surrey and Kent and invaded the Jutish Kingdom of Wight. The fighting was bitter. King Arvold of the Wight was killed and Caedwalla badly wounded. The conquest was merciless. The native population was killed, enslaved, or driven out, reduced to "wild men in the woods". When the young sons of Arvold were captured and brought before the King he ordered that they be baptized and then executed. The political geography of England was transformed. Now Wessex included Kent, Sussex and Wight, the whole south eastern coast.

## The Wight under the Kingdom of Wessex

Just two years after his conquest Caedwalla abdicated and died. The long reign of his successor, King Ine, (688-726) saw the recolonisation of the Island by Saxons and the iron-fisted conversion of the surviving pagan population as witnessed in the first known English law code "The Dooms of Ine". According to place-name evidence the new Saxon farmers first colonised the fertile Eastern Yar valley. There were also concentrations on the middle Medina, the valleys of the Western Yar and Caul Bourne, and on the south west coast. Almost all our rural place-names date from this Saxon period.

At the time of the conquest property boundaries still seem to have followed conjectural patterns from the Iron Age in which the Island was exploited in north-south strips, the fertile south used for arable and the northern forests for pasture. The new parish church divisions seem to have followed these estate lines and 1,320 years on we can still perhaps make out some of the original parish frontiers in our current local boundaries (See map). Initially there seem to have been seven parishes. Their seven churches seem to have been built on a meridian line running east to west at Brading, Newchurch, Arreton, Carisbrooke, Calbourne, Shalfleet and Freshwater. Arreton and Freshwater churches retain some Saxon stonework in their masonry. After King Ine real power passed to the Kingdom of Mercia whose great King Offa (757-796) ordered the massive 150 mile (240km) earthwork, Offa's Dyke, which physically defined the new English frontier with Wales.

## The Danish Invasion

At the end of Offa's reign Christian Europe came under a new wave of pagan attacks from the Vikings of Scandinavia. The first local raid was in 789 with just three ships. Over the next fifty years they began to arrive in fleets so powerful that they sacked Southampton in 842 and Winchester itself in 860. From 866 a "Great Army" of Danes demolished the old kingdoms one by one and then settled on their conquered lands. Only Wessex survived the onslaught under the outstanding leadership of King Alfred the Great (871-899). Alfred laid the foundations of the Kingdom of England. (He was descended on his mother's side from the old Island Jutish royal family.)

In 871 he overthrew the Danish conquest of Wessex and in 878 won a lasting victory: twenty years of peace. He used this time to reform the army and create a navy financed by taxes on fortified settlements called burghs. These became privileged markets, our first town "boroughs". Both Brading and Carisbrooke were possible Saxon burghs. Alfred's son King Edward (899-924) and his grandsons Kings Athelstan (924-939), Edmund (939-946) and Eadred (946-955) continued his policy of integrating the Danish settlers as equal citizens while expanding the power of Wessex in a series of wars of conquest of the "Danelaw" and fighting off further Viking invasions.

## The Kingdom of England

By 927 Athelstan was the first undisputed King of Anglo-Saxon England. The new kingdom reached its apogee in the peaceful reign of King Edgar (959-975) which saw a generational lull in the waves of Norse invaders. Edgar ruled a centralised English kingdom divided into counties, hundreds and parishes. His reign saw the final codification of Danish-English law, the basis of our modern law. Independent local government was assured "It is, then, my will that what you have decided for the improvement of public order, with great wisdom and in a way very pleasing to me, shall be ever observed among you." From 973 a stable

*King Alfred the Great*

uniform currency based on the penny was re-minted every seven years from 60 borough mints. The rapid circulation of the money indicates a dynamic growing national economy. State policy was discussed within the Witangehot, the precursor of the modern privy council and Parliament. The provincial rulers were the earls, (earldormen) who administered the countryside in peacetime and became regional generals of the mass army call-up (fryd) of the freemen, (ceorls) in an era of almost continuous warfare.

The highest social caste on the Island were probably the thanes, who formed the armoured core of the fryd and represented the owner/managers of the Island's agrarian estates. Around their wooden manorial great halls scattered settlements of freemen and slaves lived and worked the fields which have come to define our modern understanding of property. As population grew the original estates subdivided.

As the smaller manors became more localised, changing technology influenced the creation of our villages. The introduction of the heavy plough, which could cut a deep furrow required close co-operation between a number of households to provide the required large teams of oxen and large open fields. Households clustered together to work the land collectively. Their settlements formed the beginnings of our modern villages.

By 1066 there were 24 watermills grinding the Island's abundant corn harvest. The Saxon's open field system of agriculture would remain for a thousand years. The villages they created are still with us. On the coast, harbours developed at Brading Haven, Yarmouth-Thorley and Gurnard. Recent finds off the north-east coast have found pontoons and a fish weir near where Binstead limestone was quarried for export. In 2001 the TV Time Team uncovered the post-holes of generations of Saxon longhouses at Yaverland.

## The Fall of the House of Wessex

The dismal tale of the collapse of the House of Wessex began 90 years before the Battle of Hastings (1066). The long disastrous reign of Ethelred the Unready 978-1016 was a tragic saga of cowardice, corruption and treachery. Over mighty earls intrigued. The Viking raiders were bribed to go away, which guaranteed growing armies of invasion, which began to annihilate the uncoordinated regional English armies. From 980 the Isle of Wight was repeatedly invaded and used as a base by the over-wintering Vikings. In 999 they used the Island to launch a successful invasion of Kent. In 1013 King Sweyn drove Ethelred from the Island to join his family in exile in Normandy.

After thirty years of Danish rule, in 1042, Edward "the Confessor" the last of the House of Wessex, was re-called from Normandy to the English throne. He found the Dane Earl Godwinson was the real power in the land. King Edward had no children, and on his death, in 1066, the contest for the empty throne was between the Earl's sons Harold and Tostig, King Harold Haardrada of Norway and William Duke of Normandy, who was at least related to Edward. After the Battle of Hastings William took power. In the midwinter of 1085, almost twenty years after the Norman Conquest, King William ordered a census, down to the last plough team and slave household, of his entire kingdom. It speaks volumes of the ongoing efficiency of the Anglo-Saxon state that despite a century of government crisis, the information was collected and published at Winchester the following year. We know it as the Domesday Book.

Domesday surveys a kingdom of some two million souls, one tenth of them town dwellers; an ordered countryside of open fields, forest, and pasture; with every last unit of landed property, recorded, measured and taxed. There was an established church providing social services and education, a written English language, law code, system of weights and measures, a strong currency and a powerful sense of history. It was a united kingdom already well aware of its own sense of identity, a lasting tribute to the statesmanship of the House of Wessex.

# THE NORMAN LORDS OF THE WIGHT
## 1067-1293

For over two centuries after the Norman conquest of 1066 the Island was not directly ruled by the kings of England, but by a dynasty of semi-monarchical Norman lords. The Fitz-Osbornes 1067-1075 and the de Redvers 1101-1293 ruled the Island "as freely as the king himself held the realm of England". Their period of rule is now almost lost from history, just a few bare facts come down to us after almost one thousand years. But we do know it was a time of remarkable economic and social development, peace and prosperity, which left us a rich legacy of towns, forests, churches, further delineating the fields, parishes and roads we still use today.

*Carisbrooke Castle Keep and the high curtain walls were completed by Lord Baldwin I in the early Eleventh Century, providing an impregnable power base for the de Redvers dynasty. Courtesy of English Heritage.*

## The First Lords of the Island

When William the Duke of Normandy conquered the Anglo-Saxon Kingdom of England in 1066 almost all the counties and boroughs continued to be ruled directly by the Crown. However the Island had played such a key strategic role in the campaign of 1066 that William entrusted it to his right hand man, the Constable of Normandy, architect of the invasion, William Fitz Osbern. The first lord of the Island was killed at the Battle of Cassel in Flanders in 1071 just five years after he took ownership of the Island. However in his short reign he did refortify Carisbrooke Castle and gave the revenues of most of the Island's churches to the Abbey of Lyre, which he had founded in Normandy in 1046.

This was to be a characteristic copied by many of his contemporaries. These were violent times and the ruthless methods the Norman lords used in stabbing their way to power were typically atoned for by leaving revenues to pay generations of monks to pray for their souls in perpetuity. Much of the Island became a religious tax farm over the next two centuries. The second lord was William's son, Roger de Breteuil, but his reign was equally violent and brief. As one of the leaders of the baronial revolt of 1075 he was stripped of the lordship in 1078 and spent the rest of his long life in miserable imprisonment.

From 1078 to 1101 the Island was ruled directly by Kings William I (1066-1087) and his second son William II (1087-1100). According to custom the eldest son Robert should have succeeded William I in both the Duchy of Normandy and the Kingdom of England but William I gave him Normandy only, England to William II and nothing but ambition to his third son Henry. In August 1100 while Robert was still leading the army of Normandy back from the First Crusade, King William II was hunting in the New Forest with Henry when he was suspiciously killed by an arrow through the head. Henry immediately galloped to Winchester to seize power over England. For the next six years Henry and Robert fought for ultimate control of both England and Normandy. The Island again became strategically vital and in 1101 Henry I (1100-1135) revived the Lordship and granted it to one of his most trusted knights, Richard de Redvers, nephew of William Fitz-Osbern. Richard de Redvers, third Lord of the Island (1101-1107) was mainly pre-occupied with the war which ended with the invasion of Normandy and the final defeat of Robert in 1106.

## Baldwin de Redvers

The coat of arms of
The de Redvers family.
Courtesy of English Heritage.

The fourth Lord of the Island, Baldwin I (1107-1155), must rank as the greatest of the male line of de Redvers. By about 1135 he had founded the Island's first planned town at Yarmouth, founded the Island's greatest religious institution, Quarr Abbey and rebuilt the castle at Carisbrooke into an impregnable fortress. These were massive building projects. The castle alone required building a huge mound on Fitz Osbern's enclosure on top of which rose the stone keep that still dominates the skyline. Around the quadrangular Saxon earthworks curtain walls of hewn stone towered over the enclosed courtyard, as they still stand today.

Next to the stone quarry at Binstead, Quarr Abbey was founded in 1132, with a dozen Norman Cistercian monks who began to tame the northern forest and with the adherence of lay members, cultivated a new farmed area. Meanwhile the manor farms prospered under de Redvers neighbours from the Cotentin Peninsular of Normandy, among them the de Vernons and de Bournevilles of Chale (founded as a parish in 1114), the de Trenchards of Shalfleet, the de Lestre of Niton, the d'Oglandres of Nunwell, the de Sturs and the de Insular. By 1156 four Norman priories had been built and manned by Norman monks to manage the complex church taxes dedicated to the Norman abbeys.

In 1135 the peace of the Island was disrupted when King Henry I died and his nephew Stephen seized the throne from Henry's daughter Matilda. Baldwin unlike most of the other English barons supported Matilda and, by his capture of Exeter that year triggered a nineteen year civil war. Overwhelmed by Stephen at Exeter, Baldwin fell back to the impregnable Carisbrooke Castle only to be forced to surrender by an extraordinary drought which dried the castle well. Baldwin fled to France to return to Wareham in 1139 and to fight through to the siege of Winchester in 1141. That year a defeated Stephen restored Baldwin's title to the Island and the Wight seems to have been spared the worst of the dreadful scenes that followed in the 1140s as the civil war degenerated into baronial anarchy. "You might behold villages of famous names standing empty" wrote a monk of Winchester in 1143 "fields whitened with the harvest as the year verged upon autumn, but the cultivators had perished by famine and the ensuing pestilence."

Although the Island fares badly in international wars, where it is on the front line, it is relatively sheltered during periods of civil war. In 1154, with the death of Stephen and the accession of King Henry II the Island appears to have emerged from the long civil war unscathed and Baldwin had added a new title, Earl of Devon.

In 1155 Baldwin was buried at Quarr to be succeeded by his son Lord Richard II who died in France in 1162. His son Lord Baldwin II was also preoccupied with his lands in France where he won a wife and chateau fighting with King Henry II. He died childless in 1188. Baldwin's brother Lord Richard III 1188-1293 also died childless but his name is linked to the other great achievement of the twelfth century, the building of Newport.

The massive task of constructing the castle, importing Binstead limestone via the head of the Medina inevitably led to the construction of wharfage and accommodation for the small armies of feudal slaves and craftsmen required. Around 1120 the Priory of St Cross was built including a water mill at the junction of the Lukely and the Medina, in what became one corner of the new planned town of Newport. Around 1180 a magnificent new church was consecrated in the name of the recently murdered Archbishop of Canterbury, Thomas Beckett. Its bells would ring out over the Medina valley for the next 800 years, until its replacement in the reign of Queen Victoria.

On the death of Lord Richard III, without a legitimate son, his uncle William, the youngest brother of Baldwin I became the eighth Lord and fifth Earl. William de Redvers carefully ruled the Island through the disastrous reigns of kings Richard I (1189-1199) and John (1199-1216). These two brothers bankrupted the kingdom and dismally failed to prevent the French King Phillip capturing Normandy and eventually invading England itself. William de Redvers faithfully supported them and John based himself at Yarmouth in 1201, 1206 and 1214 to prepare his forces in the Solent before he had established the new naval base at Portsmouth, founded in 1212. The lack of other references to the Island in this renewed period of chaotic baronial rebellion and anarchy suggests the Wight was again unmolested, apart from by the stationing of some of John's mercenary soldiers.

At the height of the fighting in England William de Redvers retired to die at Quarr, leaving his grandson Lord Baldwin III (1217-1244) to pick his way through the early years of the disastrous reign of King Henry III (1216-1272). Baldwin III married the daughter of the Duke of Gloucester and they had two children who survived to adulthood, Baldwin and Isabella. Baldwin IV became the tenth Lord of the Wight from 1244. Baldwin IV's rule was complicated by the intensifying struggle between King Henry III and the baronial and Parliamentary opposition led by Simon de Montfort. In the summer of 1262 the two rival governments summoned their supporters to St Albans (de Montfort) and Windsor (Henry). Richard Earl of Gloucester and Baldwin de Redvers tried to moderate the two sides. In July they both died of poisoning at the home of Baldwin's brother-in-law, Peter de Savoy and the civil war erupted. The Island passed at this treacherous time to Isabella, Baldwin's sister.

## Isabella de Fortibus

Isabella de Fortibus is in many ways the Island's most extraordinary and tragic ruler (1262-1293). Widowed at 23, Lady of the Island at 25, this strong-willed woman hung on to the family title for the whole of the rest of her life, although all five of her children died before her. She is remarkable in that she made Carisbrooke her main residence, in her time many of the inner buildings were initially constructed. She also took the generous step of granting the burghers of Newport the freehold of their previously rented plots.

*This stone carved head of Isabella de Fortibus found at her priory at Christchurch is the only facial record we have of any of the de Redvers dynasty.*

*The likeness of Adam de Compton from Freshwater Church drawn by Percy Stone in the Nineteenth Century.*

The wheel of history had turned. The independent Lordship was now an anachronism and the new King Edward I (1272-1307) was determined to reunify the Wight with the English crown. In 1285 he seized the manor of Swainston including Newtown from the Bishop of Winchester and fined him to boot. When he heard Isabella was on her death bed in 1293 he despatched three bishops to persuade her to sell him the Island. The Earldom of Devon passed to her nearest relations, but Edward had ensured the strategic Isle was back as Crown property, which it has remained ever since.

*The Town seal of Yarmouth, then known as Eremue, The first town to be formally founded as a borough on the Island. Courtesy of Yarmouth Town Trust.*

The slight historic record left by the de Redvers is an indication of the peace and progress which took place on the Island. "Nothing mean, unknightly or profligate is recorded of any of the de Redvers". We also need to remember that these Lords of the Wight were also the Earls of Devon, had a major role to play in the court politics of the kingdom of England and held extensive territories in France. If we take the example of Devon, there were just four towns recorded in Domesday, 1086. By 1238 eighteen towns are recorded. The 1136 description of the Island as a subsistence economy "producing little corn" would be unrecognisable by the accession of Isabella de Fortibus in 1262.

The era of the de Redvers saw the extension of the agricultural area, new parishes and manors founded, new water and wind-mills to pound and grind the corn and wool that was exported in increasing volumes through the four northern ports, Yarmouth, Newtown (founded 1256 by the Bishop of Winchester) Newport and Brading. Stone churches replaced wood. Fishponds and rabbit warrens augmented the diet which included all the major crops and farm livestock that would still be familiar in the nineteenth century.

The scale of the export of rabbit meat was such that a merchant visited weekly, incidentally starting up the first known cross-Solent postal service. It was not just agriculture; the Island was also becoming the centre of an important textile manufacturing industry based on milled beaten woven wool called "kerseys". The towns allowed the English-speaking serfs to replace slavery with the freedom as burghers in the new towns. They could become specialist food processors, craftsmen, traders, manufacturers and merchants.

The population seems to have roughly quadrupled from a low figure of about 1,000 at the time of Domesday, 1086. For almost two centuries, 1101-1293, among the most violent in England's internal history, the de Redvers dynasty insulated the Island from civil war and anarchy. Although distracted by their other interests their period of wise rule saw sustained economic and social progress. Looking back these were prosperous years for the Islanders although their standard of living was wretched by our standards.

The following three centuries would be an era of constant threat of invasion, economic depression and social stagnation. Not until after 1600 would the Island begin to expand again.

# THE ISLAND'S OLDEST LIGHTHOUSE

*The ruin of St Catherine's Oratory Lighthouse. Courtesy of Dr Robin McInnes OBE.*

Close to the 780 foot high peak of the down above the roaring ocean beating Rocken End, at the south west point of the Island, stands a solitary medieval tower, St Catherine's Oratory. It is the most remote habitation of the medieval Catholic Church on the Island, the remains of the second oldest lighthouse in Britain and an edifice of another age and way of thinking. A legal case related to its founding throws a sudden passing light on one of the most obscure periods and places of English history, the Back of the Wight in the early Fourteenth Century.

## *Voyage to Oblivion*

On April 20th 1313 the trading ship the *St Marie de Bayonne* was struggling in difficult weather off the south west corner of the Isle of Wight. The sailing ship was from Bayonne, in the Basque speaking part of the Duchy of Aquitaine which was ruled by England's Plantagenet kings from 1151. She was engaged in the busy trade taking southern wine to the manufacturing region of Flanders. On this occasion she was well off course on her voyage from Tonnay on the Charente estuary in Gascony to Dieppe. She was likely pulled into the Bay by the incoming tide when fog often obscured the towering cliffs in white cloud. Her bottom grounded in Chale Bay and the waves smashed against the stricken hull. Soon her crew began to abandon the ship for the nearby shore.

Above the shore the narrow chines cut into the cliff were already busy with local armed men descending to the beach. The tough people of the scattered settlements of the "Back of the Wight" were always ready for a shipwreck. This area of the Island was the most isolated from the seat of authority in Carisbrooke Castle. The locals supplemented their meager incomes with salvage. For them the wreck of the *St Marie* was a massive opportunity as the ship was loaded with a valuable cargo, 174 barrels of fine white wine. Coming ashore here was risky for the crew. The locals were both terrorised by pirates and practised piracy themselves. It was not unknown for them to murder shipwrecked sailors so that their goods and cargo could be stolen with no-one the wiser. In 1224 the Bishop of Winchester had ordered all the churches on the Island to preach three times a year against this crime, on pain of excommunication. As other cases prove, piratic attacks on ships, even those not wrecked formed part of a regional economy of wreck, theft and salvage.

In 1231 a ship owned by Osbert Percehays had been driven to take shelter "near Freshwater". She was not a real wreck, but a crowd of local men had seized the ship and stolen the entire cargo, made up of a species of parasitic eels that predated the dinosaurs, called lampreys, which were a delicacy of the time.

## Drunken Robbery

On the night of April 20th, there was no murder, just robbery. The locals helped the crew ashore and concentrated on with the immediate salvage of the barrels. As the hull of the *St Mary* broke up in the surf a total of 150 barrels, some only half full were beached at various points along Chale Bay. The cargo still legally belonged to the owners but Islanders were long accustomed to taking shipwreck and salvage as part of their illegitimate income. Walter de Goditon, lord of Chale, accompanied by a gang of local strong men, arrived at the scene of drunken lawlessness and took the largest bulk of the rescued wine from the drenched crew.

## The King's Law

*King Edward II*

They probably did not expect to hear any more of the event. For the centuries that the Island had been ruled by the de Redvers dynasty, shipwreck had been split between the Lords of the Island and the local landlords whose domains bordered the sea. Apart from the incident with the lampreys there is a suspicious lack of any legal record of shipwreck in this feudal Island where the County Coroner was also the Constable of the Castle, directly under the Lord.

However in 1293 Edward I had purchased the Island from the dying Isabella de Fortibus and he and his successors expected and enacted rigorous royal justice. King Edward II was petitioned by the owners of the lost wine: Elie Byger, Frederick Campanare and Bernard Columers were all Gascons and therefore subjects of Edward (who was also the Duke of Gascony).

The case was prepared against four identified offenders and opened in Southampton on June 8th before an Island jury. However the four charged men, Walter de Goditon, Richard de Hogheton, Ralph de Wolverton and John Sysem refused to appear. Their attorneys John de Erle and Stephen L'Orfevre calmly lied that the "accused denied being at Chale on that day in that year." The case moved on to Winchester, to the King's residence at Westminster and back to Winchester. By this time the four felons had admitted their part. Walter de Goditon, the main offender said he had bought 53 barrels and a pipe of wine from the shipwrecked crew. The others admitted taking a barrel or two each. Sentence was handed down on February 27th 1314.

The court took control of the goods of Goditon, Wolverton and Hogheton and imprisoned John Sysem as he presumably had no property worth seizing. Their fines varied from five and a half marks for Wolverton to 287 and a half marks for Goditon. Goditon was allowed to keep his plough teams until the debt was paid and his lands returned. It would take several more cases before the royal law ran on this coast. Just a few years later, in 1320, fifty more locals were charged with "misuse of wrecked goods" from the *St Mary de Santander*. Six of them refused to appear and were declared outlaws. In 1335 and 1336 two more large wrecks were followed by organised robbery. Forty-five men from as far afield as Christchurch and Portsmouth were accused of looting the *Ship of Jesus Christ*. In the succeeding decades of the Hundred Years War (1338-1453) open piracy returned.

# "Sacrilege"

With the end of the trial in 1314 Walter de Goditon may have thought that his troubles were over, but according to local folklore there was a lot more in store. The story goes that the case of the missing wine had come to the attention of another figure, far more powerful than even King Edward. In Medieval Europe there were two authorities, the hereditary states of the king, and the universal Catholic Church ruled by Pope Clement V. The Catholic Church was at the peak of its powers in the thirteenth and then fourteenth centuries.

It was a highly centralised bureaucracy jealous to defend its privileges. It owned much of the Island directly. Its monks and priests were the literate class who managed much of the land, registered the population, recorded the law, collected taxes and provided the only official news, social welfare and education service. New parish churches were appearing all over the Island. Chale Church had been consecrated in 1114 under the mother church of Carisbrooke.

The wine that was stolen from Chale beach had been bound for the monastery of Livers in Picardy. Walter was brought before the separate church courts to be accused of "Sacrilege" (about 1303 this was defined as the crime of "stealing what is consecrated to God"). He was threatened with being sent to Hell and ordered to make a penance, to maintain a lighthouse on the "Montem de Cheal" with a chantry where a priest would live to keep the light, and maintain masses for the soul of Walter, his family and the souls of those lost at sea. Walter had to set aside rents to fund this "in perpetuity"

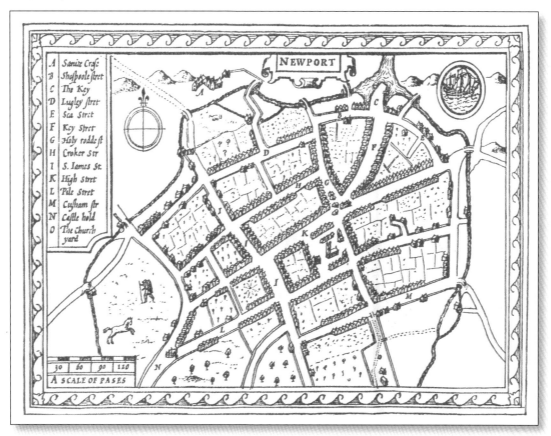

*Speed's Map of Newport in 1610 shows the planned medieval layout of the streets unchanged after 500 years.*
*Courtesy of the Isle of Wight County Records Office.*

# St Catherine's Oratory

There was already an oratory founded on the peak of the down. The fact it had been there some time is shown by the order for its repair in October 1312. The building was dedicated to St Catherine, an Egyptian who had opposed the pogrom of Christians by Emperor Maximinus (ruled 305-313) and was imprisoned and beheaded. She became a very popular saint during and after the crusades. In 1327 Walter died and the following year St Catherine's Oratory was complete. The four-storey lighthouse stood thirty-five and a half feet high (10.67m), "octangular without and quadrangular within". Next to it stood the adjoining chantry where a lone cleric lived, mass was said, and fuel was collected for the light.

Five centuries on Fred Mew writing *Back of the Wight* mused "On this desolate and windswept spot, far from other habitations, and usually shrouded in dense fog one marvels at the piety of these priests and monks who kept watch and ward there over the centuries, and the devotion which inspired them to do it." In 1438 the responsibility of maintaining "divine office at the little oratory and the lamp at night for mariners in danger" passed to Barton Oratory near Newport. In recognition for this the archpriest of Barton had to offer 2lb of wax to the Lady Altar at Carisbrooke Church during the annual Feast of the Assumption. This was perhaps in recognition of the value of the surrounding sheep grazing land. The property of the oratory was taken over by St Mary's College Winchester the following year and rented out for twenty shillings a year.

From this time there is no further record of divine services or a light, so the chantry possibly fell into disuse. It was definitely closed after Henry VIII dissolved the monasteries in 1536. As time passed the chantry disappeared leaving only the gutted stone tower. In the Eighteenth Century Sir Richard Worsley of Appuldurcombe had the four massive buttresses added to prevent the tower falling down. The 1780s also saw the attempt to build a second St Catherine's Lighthouse close by. As the old lighthouse was known locally as "The Pepperpot" the new half complete lighthouse was nick named "The Salt Shaker". It became apparent that the site was far too often foggy to be useful for a lighthouse and the work was abandoned. Only the foundation stones of the second lighthouse now remain. It would be 1840 before the third and present lighthouse was built at sea level at St Catherine's Point.

*The abandoned town of Newtown with the urban plots and wide streets grassed over is a testament to the "Disastrous Fourteenth" Century that followed on the building of the Oratory. The Island was affected by a global fall in temperatures which led to extreme weather and lost harvests. The widespread famine conditions were made worse by the outbreak of the Hundred years War from 1324. In 1349 a weakened sick population was perhaps halved by the Black death, a plague that swept across Europe. In 1377 in the greatest French attack on the island, all three Island towns were burned to the ground and Newtown, perhaps the largest, was never to recover. The combined effects of the these disasters were significant depopulation and economic decline. The Island continued to stagnate through the late Plantagenet and Tudor periods, taking about 200 years to recover.*

# THE BATTLE OF PORTSMOUTH: 1545

On July 18th 1545 a huge French invasion fleet dropped anchor from St Helens to Culver Cliff. The following day, as the English and French navies fought and manoeuvred in the Spithead, the vanguard of the French army splashed ashore in four major attacks along the length of the eastern coast of the Island. Bloody fighting ensued. The Battle of Portsmouth witnessed the last invasion of the Isle of Wight and the tragic loss of the King's Ship, *Mary Rose*. In the event the battle was not won by the superbly equipped English navy, but by the civilian army of Island militia, stabbing and hacking with billhooks and daggers, driving the armoured invaders back into the sea.

*This copy of the Cowdray engraving shows a part of the Battle of Portsmouth looking south over Southsea and Spithead to the Eastern end of the Isle of Wight. On the left is the French invasion fleet moored off the Island. The topmasts of the Mary Rose can be seen poking above the waves in front of Southsea castle where King Henry VIII was watching the battle.*
*"Oh my pretty men" he was heard to exclaim, "drowned like rattens". Courtesy of Portsmouth City Museum.*

In 1545 the Kingdom of England was ruled by the aging King Henry VIII (1509-1547). Throughout his reign Henry had poured gold and resources into armaments, warships and the army. In 1538 he had used the Protestant Reformation (1517-) to seize personal control of the church in England in order to marry his second wife. The Pope demanded his overthrow and Henry knew it was only a matter of time before France or Spain invaded. The dissolved Catholic monasteries, like Quarr Abbey, had their stone ransacked for the biggest coastal castle building programme since the late-Roman "Forts of the Saxon Shore" 1200 years before. Using modern ballistic technology these castles were constructed as impregnable stone cannon-platforms designed primarily to blast enemy warships out of the water. Hurst Castle, Worsley's Tower and the Sharpnode Blockhouse guarded the treacherous narrow western entrance to the Solent. Other castles and fortifications dominated the main anchorages and passages; Calshot, Hasleworth, Yarmouth, Cowes, East Cowes, Portsmouth and Southsea. The vulnerable east coast of the Island was defended by Sandham Castle in Sandown Bay and St Helens fort.

In 1544 Henry made an alliance with Spain and attacked France, an English army capturing Boulogne. The French King, Francis I (1515-1547) immediately made peace with Spain to concentrate on retribution against Henry. He decided to capture the principal English naval base, Portsmouth. The English position was perilous, with armies and ships fighting as far afield as France, Ireland and Scotland (Edinburgh fell to the English in 1544). Henry called all available remaining resources to the defence of Portsmouth. However many of the new fortresses were not yet finished and the French forces massing at Le Harvre easily beat off the English fleet when it attacked in June.

In the summer of 1545, like the summer of 1940, Islanders looked out to sea with a constant awareness of the imminent threat of violent invasion. Across the Channel a French host of 30,000 troops and an armada of over 200 warships were preparing to attack the Solent. On our hilltops, militia troops stood on 24 hour guard, ready to fire the two dozen invasion beacons that would alert the whole of southern England. It was like 1940, but this time it happened.

## The French Armada sails

In mid July, Claude D'Annebault Admiral of France, set sail aboard *La Maitresse* to lead the French armada across the Channel. It was a massively powerful fleet, with 150 large warships and 50 smaller warships and troop transports. Most importantly for the coming battle he had 25 galleys, slave powered, oar-driven warships from the Mediterranean, each mounted with a single powerful cannon in the bow. D'Annebault's 30,000 troops were not only intended to fight on land. Naval warfare was still largely a matter of ramming and boarding. The main warships had wooden castle towers on fore and aft bristling with anti-personnel guns, archers and soldiers. At the same time large cannon were being mounted inside the hulls of the large warships, firing through gunports. (It is this mixture of Medieval and modern naval warfare that best explains the tragic loss of the *Mary Rose*.)

Henry and the Privy Council arrived at Portsmouth on the 15th. The national network of beacons flared across the country. Reinforcements poured in from land and sea. The English fleet grew from 60 to 105 warships as the battle progressed while thousands of militia marched south under the hot summer sun. The professional army under Charles Brandon gathered at Southsea where many boarded the warships in the harbour for the expected naval battle. Brandon had about 12,000 troops and militia at his disposal. On July 18th, the French fleet could be seen, a growing forest of masts. Henry watched from Southsea Castle as the two fleets deployed in the light winds and engaged in a thundering cannonade.

## The Battle Begins

During this first day of the battle the English were driven back but a decisive full-scale battle was impossible. The disparity in numbers meant the English could not fight the French on the open sea. They hoped to lure them into the shallows and narrow channels of the Spithead, where they could be destroyed in detail. The French were wary of the Spithead sandbanks. They needed to provoke the English to attack them in the more open waters where they could be encircled and annihilated. Frustrated by the superb defensive position of the English forces, the best option for stimulating an English attack was to invade the Island, burning buildings and crops right in front of Henry. As the inconclusive fighting of the 18th ended the French commanders drew up their plans.

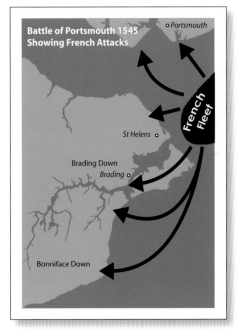

Battle of Portsmouth 1545
Showing French Attacks

Portsmouth

French Fleet

St Helens

Brading Down

Brading

Bonniface Down

In 1545 the population of the Island was about 9,000 people mostly living in scattered rural settlements. Thanks to the fighting of the Hundred Years War they lived in a highly militarised society, with weekly, compulsory, military training. The Island was split into ten Centons, each responsible for raising a company of troops. The entire male adult population was obliged to serve and some women fought as archers.

The Captain of the Island was Sir Richard Worsely of Appuldurcombe, a "capable and energetic commander". (Sheridan) He commanded about 6,000 Island, Hampshire and Wiltshire militia. Worsely was also assisted by a professional field commander. Sir Edward Bellingham who brought with him the equivalent of a headquarters staff. On the day of the invasion 850 Wiltshire militia guarded the forts of the West Wight and the critical route to Lymington where further reinforcements waited. 250 men were labourers working on the incomplete castle at Sandown. Worsely

*The King's Ship Mary Rose at sea. Courtesy of The Mary Rose Trust.*

concentrated the companies of Island militia into a small field army which occupied positions below the summit of Brading Down. C. T. Witherby estimated this force at 3,000 men. The bulk of the 2,800 Hampshire companies took up a similar position under Boniface Down. Compared to the heavily armoured French troops, bristling with the latest firearms and steel blades, the militia relied on long pikes topped with a bill- hook, and daggers, knives and clubs for close fighting. The Welsh longbow provided their firepower. However they had advantages in speed, agility and the sheer bloody-minded determination to defend their own homes.

## The sinking of the Mary Rose

July 19th dawned a clear summers day with light and variable winds. Again the galleys led the French attack into the Spithead. Again the English flagships, *Mary Rose* and *Henri Grace a Dieu* led the fleet out of Portsmouth and began a fierce artillery duel with the galleys. While the *Mary Rose* manoeuvred in the fighting she keeled over to port in the flukey winds, weighed down by the extra soldiers and cannon in her fighting castles. The sea poured through the open gunports and began to fill the hull. In a few moments she was gone, just her topmasts poking above the surface of the Spithead. "Oh my pretty men, oh my gentlemen" the King exclaimed "drowned like rattens" (drowned like rats). Of the 700 men believed to be aboard, only about 40 survived. The galleys also inflicted damage on the *Henri Grace a Dieu* until they were in turn attacked by English "row barges". In close fighting they forced the French galleys to retreat. Some slaves and sailors were killed or captured but at the end of the fighting neither side had lured the other into the suicidal attack necessary for a general engagement.

## The French capture of St Helens

Meanwhile D'Annebault launched a three pronged attack on the Island, at St Helens, Sandown and Bonchurch. As the three flotillas of landing craft with their escorting galleys pulled across the calm blue waters towards the Island, the English militia armies began their advance towards the likely beachheads. An Italian mercenary, Pietro Strozzi, led the attack on St Helens Fort. This fort had been bombarding the galleys attacking Portsmouth in the flank. Strozzi's men landed

*Detail of the Cowdray engraving showing the English Army camp at Southsea.*

successfully, killed the defenders and captured the fort. They then drove the remaining English forces back into the woods, killing and burning as they went. Seaview, St Helens and Nettlestone were all captured and set on fire.

## "The Battle of Bonchurch"

In the south a larger force commanded by Le Seigneur de Tais, Colonel General of the Infantry of France landed at Bonchurch. The French landed unopposed and began to advance inland, up steep thickly wooded slopes. The Hampshire companies took up a strong defensive position, flanked by cliffs and screened by woods. The first French attack was driven back but de Tais rallied his men. He organised them into "array" fighting formation and attacked again. After a vicious fight, with heavy loss on both sides the English line broke. Retreat turned into a rout as the militia fled the battle. One Captain Fischer who was too overweight to run cried out offering £100 for anyone who could bring him a horse. "but none could be had even for a kingdom" Fischer was either killed where he stood or captured and buried at sea, as he was never heard of again.

## The Battle of Sandown

The third French attack pulled across Sandown Bay to attack the incomplete castle. They were led by the galley captains Marsay and Pierrebon. This attack was the most critical of the three. Had the French mounted the shallow cliffs they could easily deploy on the flat countryside to split the English army in two and move inland. Reinforcements could move in all directions, south to complete the destruction of the Hampshire companies, or north or west to the Island's towns of Brading and Newport.

Worsley and Bellingham seem to have recognised the danger. The main Island army advanced so rapidly that the French seem to have barely had the chance to get organised on the beach. A hail of English arrows fell on the French. Hundreds, then thousands of men were soon fighting on the cliffs and beaches around the beleaguered castle. Formations of pikemen clashed together, as fighting in formation descended into one-to-one armed combat. Both Marsay and Pierrebon were wounded and carried away from the fighting. Leaderless, the French fell back onto their boats and pushed them out to sea, leaving the jubilant victorious English to strip the French corpses of their valuable arms and armour.

# The Struggle for the East Wight

From this point D'Annebault's plan continued to go horribly wrong. The troops of the second wave of attack had lost patience and landed without a commander on the "isle" of Bembridge, then connected to the rest of the Island by a single bridge at Yaverland. They fanned across the peninsula burning houses and farm buildings. Worsley and Bellingham now moved their field army across the Yar bridge and up the slope of Culver Down. Realising the importance of mobility and shock tactics they pulled together all their horsemen used for carrying messages and unlimbered the horses of the baggage train to form a body of improvised cavalry. As the French soldiers climbed to the summit of Culver Down they saw the Island army come galloping and charging towards them. Worsley's charge cleared the top of the down and routed the French all the way back to the ruins of Bembridge.

There the French infantry held off the attack at a hedge and ditch defence line. D'Annebault recalled du Tais from Bonchurch to sort out this escalating mess, as increasing numbers of his troops joined this unofficial battle. The Islanders withdrew back to the Yar and cut the bridge as the French advanced again to occupy the whole Isle of Bembridge. Later as du Tais organised the retreat of the forces at Bembridge the Islanders attacked again, finally driving the invaders back into the sea. This seems to mark the end of the day's fighting.

The French remained in the area for some days but the simple fact that the battle was a stalemate could not be avoided. D'Annebault did consider the occupation of the Island "having it under our control, we could then dominate Portsmouth... and so put the enemy to extraordinary expense in maintaining a standing army and navy to contain us." (Martin du Bellay). The idea was abandoned when it was realised that the armada lacked sufficient engineers and logistics for the necessary fortifications.

## The French admit defeat

Before the French finally left the south of the Island they were to suffer one last humiliation. One of the galley commanders, the Chevalier d'Aulps, Pierre de Blacas landed to collect water. To protect his men he led a party up a nearby hill to watch for the enemy. There they were attacked by the militia. As his men fled, De Blacas was brought down by an arrow in his knee. Then he was struck on the head by a billhook. This knocked off his helmet. He called out for "ransom" (a large payment for the man who captured him). His adversary clearly did not care for the etiquette of courtly warfare. He "dashed out his brains, which was a great loss to the king's service, for he was a right valiant and experienced gentleman." (du Bellay)

The frustrated French armada raised anchor and sailed on to attack Shoreham in Sussex before returning to France. Henry and Francis made peace the following year at the Treaty of Ardres. Boulogne was restored to France. There are few mementoes of these long forgotten battles on the Island, the castle at Sandown is far under the sea along with much of the coastline of the time.

However there is one amazing time capsule. If you visit the Mary Rose Museum in Portsmouth you can see the 19th of July 1545, for yourself; the weapons, clothes, utensils, medicines and games of 560 years ago; on the day the countrymen of Wight saved the reputation of the King of England.

*Personal Possessions of the crew of the Mary Rose preserved for half a Millennia in the Spithead silt and now on display with The Mary Rose Trust.*

27

# THE ISLAND & FOUNDING OF THE USA

Four hundred years ago, in 1607, the first permanent English colony was established on mainland America. From this tiny beginning the United States of America trace their origin. The Isle of Wight played an intimate role in this world-changing enterprise, as Cowes Roads was the launch pad of the English expeditions. On May 14th 1607 Christopher Newport's ships the *Susan Constant, Godspeed* and *Discovery* dropped anchor some forty miles up the Powhaten River, 60 miles from the mouth of Chesapeake Bay on the east coast of North America. They had endured a dreadful transatlantic journey of 144 days during which forty men and boys had died. But this was just a foretaste of the sheer misery to come. Over the next twenty years the migrants fought a desperate struggle for survival to maintain the first permanent English settlement in mainland America. Adventurous Islanders were at the forefront of this perilous enterprise, as sailors, investors, merchants and colonists. In recognition of their contribution the County of the Isle of Wight was created in 1634.

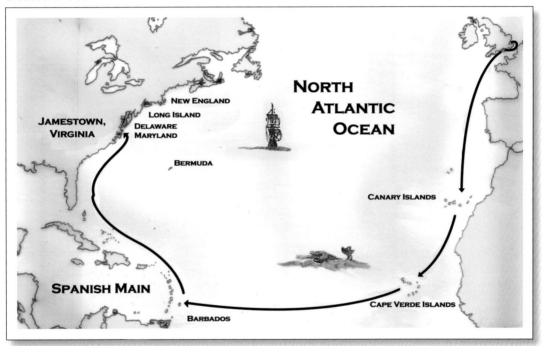

It was not until the 1580s, almost a century after Columbus discoveries of the Americas, that the English attempted a permanent settlement of their own in The "New World". Sir Walter Raleigh sponsored a company to colonise an area that was called "Virginia" named in honour of his Queen Elizabeth I (1558-1603). The first colony was established in 1585. The English had little success in this hostile, strange environment. The first expedition was rescued the following year. In 1587 a second group of 144 colonists were deposited. After the interruption of the Spanish Armada (1588) the relief ships did not reach them until 1590 by which time all the colonists had vanished.

In June 1606 the Virginia Company was revived as a joint stock company with shareholders. Each share promised 100 acres of America, plus 50 more acres for every man they transported. In 1607 two expeditions, one from Plymouth and one from London, established new settlements in New England and Virginia. The Plymouth venture failed in the first year but at Jamestown the 105 settlers built a fort around a barn and some huts and clung on for dear life.

# Early Jamestown: Saved by Nicotine

Jamestown was situated in a damp swampy country that did not suit the health of the settlers. Once the ships returned to England the colonists suffered terrible hardships. Modern archaeology shows them living in conditions akin to the Dark Ages a thousand years before, eking out a living in straw roofed huts. In the first year they were saved by Captain John Smith who developed good relations with the local native Americans. After Captain Smith left with the next convoy in 1609 the first Anglo-Powhaten War broke out with the native Americans and the colonists had to endure "The Starving Time". On June 6th 1610, the remaining 60 emaciated survivors of the 500 settlers who had made the various landings up to that point, had already abandoned the town when they met the next relief convoy carrying their first Governor, Lord De La Warr. The new governor, who became known locally as "Delaware" vigorously campaigned to destroy the Powhaten's villages and crops.

The war ended in 1613 with the marriage of one of the settlers, John Rolfe, with the fabled Powhaten Princess Pocahontas. John Rolfe's greater contribution to the colony was his adaptation of tobacco plants. In 1616 the first tobacco was exported. From that moment the future of the struggling colony was assured. It was reckoned to require six times less labour than any other crop and commanded a high price as nicotine addiction gripped Europe. By 1617 it was growing in the streets of Jamestown. As the crop exhausted the land in three years the tiny town was now bound to expand.

# The Isle of Wight Plantation

From the very beginning the Isle of Wight was intimately involved in the Virginian venture. The London convoys used Cowes Roads as their point of departure, south west to the Canaries, on to the Cape Verde Islands and west to Barbados, before finally reaching Virginia. Islanders were involved as seamen and suppliers of gathering convoys and as colonists and company investors. In 1618 two of the Island's leading figures, the baron Sir Richard Worsley, and the Newport merchant Robert Newland received a royal patent to found a plantation with seven other shareholders including a Protestant dissenter Captain Christopher Lawne.

Captain Lawne set out with about one hundred settlers on the *Marygold* arriving at Jamestown on the 27th April 1619. Lawne founded the plantation southeast of Jamestown in the country of the Warraskoyak people. It was first known as the Warraskoyak's Plantation. In July Captain Lawne was delegated to represent the plantation at the General Assembly at Jamestown. This was the first gathering of free men under English law in America. It founded a democratic tradition that would eventually create the USA. By November 1619 Christopher Lawne was dead and the plantation shareholders were asked to find more settlers. Their new charter stipulated that their land "shall henceforth be called the "Ile of Wights Plantacon". However the old native name remained in use until the 1630s. Among the shareholders Richard Wiseman owned the 350 ton *Abigail* which sailed back and forth with migrants and tobacco.

Robert Newland had a ship and a dock built at East Cowes to take advantage of what was now clearly a profitable trade. Despite the staggering death rate the new colony offered the young a sense of opportunity. On February 11th 1621, in old St. Thomas' Church in Newport, the marriages of a number of young people were recorded with a note adding "Last fyve cupples were for Virginia".

# War of Extermination

By 1622 the Jamestown colony had grown to 1,240 settlers, now spreading out along the estuaries of the James River. This was too much for the various local peoples. They formed a secret agreement and in a in a ferocious co-ordinated attack 347 English settlers were slaughtered, 55 at the Isle of Wight Plantation.

In 1623 a further 26 of the plantation's colonists died of the mixture of war and starvation. According to one they died "miserablie through nastines & many [departed] the World in their owne dung for want of help in their sicken".

By 1624 the Plantation had been reduced to thirty to fifty survivors in three households. In April 1623 a fort was built for the plantation and in July English forces attacked, burning the native corn crops and settlements and putting anyone they found to the sword. By the 1640s the Warraskoyaks had been completely driven out of what now became known as Isle of Wight County. Like so many Indian nations after them they ceased to exist as a group away from their land. They paid a terrible price for our successful colonisation. In the US 2000 census only 0.26% of the current population of Isle of Wight County are defined as "native".

## Isle of Wight County

1619 not only saw the first General Assembly, but also the first shipload of wives for sale, and more ominously, the first sale of 20 black slaves, a foretaste of the human flood of misery to come. The first shipload of 90 young unmarried women landed at Jamestown sold as brides for 125 pounds of tobacco each. These were women who had fallen on hard times. Take young Elizabeth Baker of Newport. In 1624, with the consent of her widowed mother her uncle, innkeeper John Kent, signed the contract of her sale. He paid £6 for her crossing to the ship's master who placed her with Messrs Blackwell and Cheeseman of Newport Newes. Their role was to marry off Elizabeth and in return send John Kent "six score pounds of good merchantable Virginia tobacco." Many more went out as "indentured labourers" sentenced to work for their masters without pay or freedom for a fixed penalty of years. These British semi-slaves were eventually replaced by African chattel slaves.

After the war, in 1634, Isle of Wight County was established as one of the first eight "shire" counties in the Americas, complete with Lord Lieutenant, sheriffs, bailiffs and a vote for every free man. With peace came prosperity. The population grew from 522 in 1635 to 2,019 in 1658.

In 1632 St Lukes church was founded and built with local clay bricks and oyster shell cement. It is the oldest existing church of English foundation in America, and the USA's only original gothic building. By 1750, Jamestown itself had vanished under the fields but Isle of Wight and five of the other original counties still remain. The County now has 30,000 people living on 820 square kilometres with a very proud history.

*St Lukes Church in Isle of Wight County Virginia, is the only surviving original gothic building on the Continent and the oldest church of English foundation in the Americas.*

## Other Stories

Cowes Roads continued to be launch point of expeditions. America was attractive to people seeking religious freedom. In 1620 Protestant families fleeing persecution had landed in New England from Plymouth. In 1633 the Catholic, Lord Baltimore, set sail from Cowes in the *Ark and the Dove* to establish the religiously tolerant "Palatinate of Maryland". A commemorative plaque was erected on the Cowes Parade in 1933 to mark the tri-centenary.

About 1639 an English settler, Lion Gardiner, visited the Isle of Manchonat off Long Island (modern New York state). He was impressed with its magnificent forests, saltwater ponds and freshwater streams. He bought all 3,000 acres from the Algonquian nation with some cloth, a gun, gunpowder and a large black dog. He recognised the island had the same shape as the Isle of Wight. The isle was for sometime known as the Isle of Wight although it officially became Gardiner's Isle.

The Americas continued to play an important role for the Island. When Dutch warships attacked Virginia in 1667 they seized twenty vessels "trading with the Isle of Wight". Right down to the 1780s Cowes acted as the international customs and clearing house for imports of rice from the Carolinas. By that time Cowes had grown from a tiny suburb of Newport into the Island's second greatest town, largely thanks to this American colonial trade.

*The port of Cowes developed largely in response to the new American trade as convoys for Virginia, Maryland, Delaware, North and South Carolina, Georgia and the Caribbean used Cowes Roads as their point of departure.*
*Courtesy of Dr Robin McInnes OBE.*

# THE ROYAL PRISONERS 1647-1653

*King Charles I 1625-1649.*
*Courtesy of English Heritage Osborne House.*

King Charles I (1625-1649) was one of the worst kings in British history. Unable to accept criticism of his policy he ruled without Parliament. Without Parliament he could not raise legal taxes. This forced him to sell off the huge royal estates that had been held here on the Island and nationally since Saxon times.

By 1642 his policies led to revolutions and civil wars in each of his three kingdoms, England, Ireland and Scotland. His deeply unpopular rule resulted on the Island in the easy overthrow of the power of the royalist garrisons in the Island's four castles during the month of August.

The Parliamentarian interest was bravely upheld by Newport Town Council, with the decisive support of the navy. Carisbrooke Castle fell to a force of 600 sailors and local militia.

Despite the clear Parliamentary sympathy of most Islanders Charles escaped here after his defeat in the First English Civil War. He was arrested and imprisoned at Carisbrooke Castle in 1647. Late in 1648 a delegation from Parliament negotiated a peace treaty with him called the Treaty of Newport. By now the leadership of the Parliamentary Army had discovered that their king had plotted with the Scots to invade England, causing the Second English Civil War. As a result the king was taken to London, put on trial for treason, and publicly beheaded in January 1649.

The year after the execution of King Charles, his daughter, Princess Elizabeth was brought to Carisbrooke where she perished soon after of influenza, no doubt made worse by being separated from the rest of her family, who were now refugees. She is interred in Sts Thomas' Church in Newport, commemorated in this beautiful memorial commissioned by Queen Victoria.

Three days after Elizabeth died the Council of State ordered her release so that she could join her sister in exile in the Netherlands. If only she had known it might have given her the will to recover? The other royal prisoner was Elizabeth's little brother Henry, Duke of Gloucester, who was imprisoned with Elizabeth and was finally released to join his family in 1653.

*Princess Elizabeth sculpted by Carlo Marochetti.*
*Photo by Rodney Hogg.*

# THE ISLAND'S LEONARDO
## Robert Hooke 1635-1703

How many people have even heard of the greatest Islander in world history? Using instruments he invented and built himself, Robert Hooke founded meteorology, geology, and micro-biology. He pioneered geography, chemistry, physics and medicine. Yet the reputation of this low-born self-made man was so buried by his rivals that he almost completely disappeared from history. It is still impossible to give a complete judgement of Robert Hooke's personal achievements. It would require a symposium of historical specialists in a score of subjects as Hooke was a polymath to whom all practical subjects were open to enquiry. Like Leonardo da Vinci, to whom he is often compared, he designed prototype flying machines as well as being a fine artist and architect. One inadequate description of this restless genius is "the inspirational father of modern science."

*Robert Hooke as a boy at Freshwater Bay by Rita Greer.*
*Courtesy of the Isle of Wight Planetarium.*

## *Rise to Prominence*

Robert Hooke was born in the humble rectory of Freshwater on July 18th 1635. Despite being poor, physically handicapped and with lifelong ill-health Hooke possessed extraordinary personal energy, outstanding technical ability and a theoretical genius. Robert Hooke grew up in an England of violent revolutionary change. When he was seven civil war broke out between King Charles I and Parliament. Following the death of his father, the thirteen year old Robert was immediately sent to London with £40 and a trunk of books to be fortuitously enrolled in Westminster School.

From Westminster School he entered Christchurch College Oxford on a poor scholars' fellowship in 1653. As a traditional career in the church was impossible in revolutionary Britain, his guardians at Westminster and Oxford, encouraged Hooke to become a technical assistant. Hooke has already shown precocious mechanical ability as a child in Freshwater. His deformed shoulders were attributed to his long hours at the workbench.

*The Island's forgotten Leonardo, Robert Hooke.*
*The last picture of Sir Robert Hooke in a stained window*
*in St Helen's Church Bishopsgate was blown out by an*
*IRA bomb in 1993.*

At Oxford Hooke was introduced to a group of natural philosophers who met weekly to discuss scientific questions. In 1657 Hooke appears to have invented the spiral spring time-piece, the basis of the modern mechanical wristwatch. However in what would be characteristic of Hooke, he never completed the work, but turned to other subjects. Only in 1675 did he publish his work to contest the claim of another inventor. One reason for this frustrating failure to finish what he started was that Hooke's life was not his own. From 1658 he was employed by the aristocratic natural philosopher Sir Robert Boyle. Together they developed "Boyle's Law of Gases". This gives the theoretical basis for James Watt's steam engine (1776) which kick-started the modern industrial world. Boyle could not operate the air pump that Hooke had built and as he was not a mathematician, the law that carries his name was more likely due to his employee.

## The Royal Society

After the restoration of the monarchy in 1660, when Hooke was 25, this Oxford group of academic aristocrats would form the Royal Society for Improving Natural Knowledge. In 1662 Hooke became Curator of Experiments of the brand new Royal Society and in 1663 he added to the status of servant when he himself was elected as a "fellow" of the Society. The Royal Society found a home at Gresham College in central London and rapidly acquired a library and specimens of scientific interest. Hooke became responsible for these and can be seen as the man who gave the Royal Society its shape and form which made it so central to the evolution of modern science from 1660. This involved a fantastic amount of work. Hooke had to demonstrate several new experiments every week for the other members to analyse. He also had to follow up the highly varied requests of the society members. This involved spreading his expertise over a vast area of practical and theoretical problems. Always obliging, he had very little time for his own work. To make matters worse the fledgling Royal Society was often unable to pay Hooke his paltry salary.

In 1664 he became Lecturer of Mechanics and in 1665 Professor of Geometry and moved into Gresham College, where he would live for the rest of his life. That year he produced his most famous work, *Micrographia*, after he built his own compound microscope and published his exquisite drawings of the world of inner space. Hooke was the first to describe the existence of microorganisms and the first to study and name "cells". At the same time he was improving telescopes and observing the heavens, publishing *Cometa* in 1666. Among his achievements he discovered the elliptical shape of the Earth and of orbits, he described the motion of the Sun among the stars, discovered sunspots, the red spot of Jupiter and that planet's rotation. Beyond the Solar System he found the fifth star of Orion and the first binary star.

## Planner and Architect

In September 1666 a fire in a bakery in Pudding Lane grew into an inferno that burned half of central London, being halted within a block of Gresham College. The refugee city authorities and merchants moved into the college and Hooke found himself at the centre of the planning for the new London. Hooke soon had the backing of the Corporation of London and the Royal Society for his proposals and was appointed as one of the six commissioners for the rebuilding.

*"Cometh the hour, cometh the man". Hooke immediately rose to the occasion after the disaster of the Great Fire of London. He is painted here by Rita Greer initiating the survey of the destroyed city. Courtesy of Isle of Wight Planetarium.*

In 1667 he was appointed Surveyor of London with the task of measuring out the new wider roads and the original property sites. He had an important influence on building regulations to ensure that the new buildings were strong and fireproof.

His work in planning led to a new career as an architect. (Finally he was getting properly paid but he still had his old jobs to do). He designed many buildings including churches, houses, the London Monument and Bethlehem mental hospital which resembled a palace. In this career he invented the modern surveyor's wheel, the cartenary curve for building steeples and the double-vaulted dome used for the new St Paul's Cathedral. Hooke's public works introduced him to a wider public. A single man, he was a great socialite, with an itinerary of 2,000 cafes and bars recorded in his diary where he saw different groups of people to discuss his and their separate interests.

## Environmentalist Visionary

In 1665 Hooke revisited the Island to sort out family affairs following the death of his mother. While he was here he took samples from the cliffs he knew so well to help him predict the modern sciences of geology, biology and geography. According to the received wisdom the world had been created as it is in 4004BC, by God, at 9.00am on October 26th. Hooke was religious, but valued rational proof before dogma. He argued for a sequence of natural processes taking vast periods of time, a dynamic Earth with a liquid molten interior causing earthquakes and volcanoes, the bottoms of oceans rising to the peaks of mountains, the geographical process of erosion, the water cycle, the petrification of fossils, the shifting of the Poles and the extinction and evolution of species through environmental change, predicting the work of Charles Darwin.

Three centuries ahead of his time, he said "the Earth we inhabit and everything about it; its air, its water, its land, and all species of life, should concern us as humans."Hooke also founded the science of Meteorology. He realised that weather was due to varying air pressure and invented the first weather station, and tools to measure it, the first anemometer, (wind speed) the hygrometer (humidity) an improved the barometer (air pressure), thermometer (temperature) and altimeter (height).

# From Fame to Obscurity

*Sir Isaac Newton once wrote to Hooke the immortal phrase "If I have seen further it is by standing on the shoulders of giants" but he never gave Hooke credit for his part in developing the theory of gravity.*

In other areas Hooke learned that sound travelled along metal wire and projected the idea of the telegraph. He established the concept of frequency for sound. He established the Law of Elasticity (1678). Among his other achievements he explained the shape of crystal, predicted the role of oxygen in respiration and combustion.

By the 1670s Hooke's health was starting to break down. He had major public disputes with several contemporaries who appeared to use his ideas but did not credit him. The most damaging dispute was with Isaac Newton. Hooke had established many of the principles of gravity long before Newton published in 1684. From 1666 Hooke suggested gravity is "an attractive property of the body placed at the centre" He specifically described "the gravitating power" that defines all the bodies observable in space, wrote of the inverse square relationship of gravity to distance and the simultaneously linear and circular motion of planets.

His predictions worked for both planets and comets. In 1679 he wrote to Newton to point out the correct direction of gravitational fall and of the existence of the balancing centripetal force without which the theory of universal gravitation would have been "inconceivable". Newton had a weakness that he could not accept criticism. He developed a bitter hatred for Hooke. Following Hooke's death in 1703 Sir Isaac Newton became the President of the Royal Society until his death in 1727. In 1710 the Royal Society moved from Gresham College. In this move Hooke's portraits, his scientific instruments, inventions and fossils all disappeared.

The sea clock he presented to the Royal Society which could have solved the problem of Longitude a century earlier, was rediscovered, uncatalogued, in Newton's old college at Cambridge in 1950. Newton even requested to have all Hooke's papers burned! Hooke was now depicted as a cantankerous, dishevelled, mischief-maker and written out of history. His role in the rebuilding of London is now credited to Sir Christopher Wren. The patterns of light refraction he described in 1665 became "Newton's Rings". The reflecting telescope he built became the "Newton Telescope". The comet he observed in 1665 and said was the same as that of 1618 was of course named "Halley's Comet" (1705). Uranus, discovered by Hooke in 1673 was more famously discovered by William Herschell in 1781. Even his corpse was exhumed, and lost.

## Epilogue

The Royal Society continues to this day, now with 120 staff rather than one. They publish the oldest scientific journal in continuous publication, started by Hooke in 1665. At first sight there is little to commemorate Robert Hooke. The road where he was born is named Hooke Hill and there is a simple monument at the bottom of the road. He has craters named after him on the Moon where he first identified and drew them and on Mars, whose rotation he was the first to measure. For years Trevor Clarke of Freshwater, who died in 2004, collected books and artefacts related to Hooke. Some of these are now on show at the IW Planetarium at Fort Victoria. For more information telephone 761555. In the meantime he is always around us. Next time you need a respirator, open a sash window, use a spirit level, lick your tooth fillings, use a calculator or camera or mechanical timepiece, wear artificial fibres, use a telephone or hearing aid, drive a car, sail a false keel boat or use sonar please remember that Hooke invented it or its prototype or some part of it, like the universal joint, without which it could not be.

# SMUGGLING IN THE WIGHT 1700-1850

Imagine a foul-weather black night on the Back of the Wight in the late 1700s. A large sailing ship noses her way carefully around the ship-killing ledges towards the towering cliffs. Aboard the blackened ship expert local pilots stare up at a coastal cottage. In a high narrow window a blue light briefly flashes to indicate the ship is "on the spot" and the "coast is clear". The ship returns a single blue "flink" of light from a spout lantern. Aboard the ship the experienced crew lower boats and ropes carrying lines of barrels as the ship gently beaches, carefully anchored so that she can be quickly winched back into deep water.

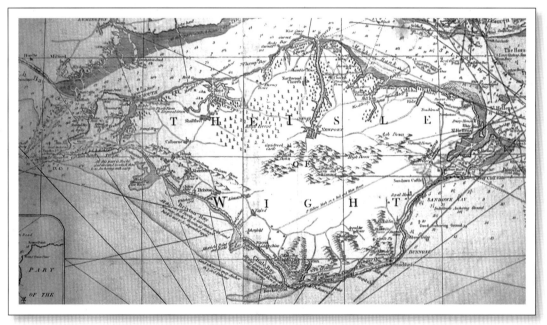

*The coastal waters of the Isle of Wight in the Eighteenth Century, the golden heyday of the smuggling industry.*
*Courtesy of the Isle of Wight County Records Office.*

*The cargo's lowered from the dark skiff's side*
*And the tow line drags the tubs thro' the tide*
*Now pray ye all that luck may bide*
*And no revenue men may this way stride*

The jagged cliffs of the chine above the shore are now alive with hundreds of men and women climbing and descending to a scene of organized chaos on the beach. Human chains stretch out to the ship, ropes of barrels are dragged ashore cut into twos and lifted on the shoulders of men who return to ascend the slippery chine. Speed is of the essence in getting thousands of gallons of concentrated alcohol and tons of tea onto the beach, up to the top of the cliff and away across the countryside before the next Revenue patrol finds them. Pack animals drawn from farms in a ten-mile radius are loaded and the cargo dispersed to a thousand secret hiding places before dawn.

*Merrily now in goodly row*
*Away, away the smugglers go*
*Threading their way through hedge and ditch*
*Though the night is dark and black as pitch*

*The Eel Pie Inn by Thomas Rowlandson. In 1791 the Island had a good range of such hostelries which catered for the growing market of mainland visitors like Rowlandson and his three friends who toured the Island that year. These inns no doubt benefited from the supplies of cheap liquor made available by the smuggling industry. Courtesy of Dr Robin McInnes OBE.*

This scene was repeated many hundreds of times, indicative of a huge illegal industry, possibly the greatest industry on the Island at the time. For one hundred and fifty years, from 1700 to 1850 virtually the entire population of the Island was directly engaged in or implicated in the criminal activity of smuggling contraband. The smugglers faced arrest, imprisonment, crippling fines, confiscation of property, transportation to Australia, compulsory service in the navy and possible execution. Yet the Islanders believed they were in the right. The smuggling laws they flouted ran against their deep seated principle of "free trade". The Golden Age of Smuggling, 1700-1815 saw the culmination of an industry already seven centuries old and still with us today. "The Golden Age" was brought about by exorbitant taxes on imports creating huge profit incentives. It came to an end after 1815 when the state finally brought sufficient forces to bear to enforce the law. It was followed by the more sophisticated "Scientific Age of Smuggling" 1815-1850. The industry finally lost purpose with the victory of the free traders in Parliament.

It had been the "custom" for wine importers to give the English kings the best of their cargo since 979AD. For as long as there have been such taxes on trade there has been smuggling. From 1275 this mostly involved the illegal export of wool to the continent. In 1689 Britain entered a 126 year period of conflict with France, Spain, and the Netherlands for control of the world's trade. Britain was officially at war for seventy of these years, wars fought in every continent, wars that were ruinously expensive. The gentry-landlord-dominated Parliament kept the land-tax low and instead piled new taxes onto luxury consumption. Taxes were levied on an amazing range of items, hats, gloves, playing cards, windows... However the most important were taxes on the drugs of pleasure, alcohol, tobacco, chocolate and tea. For example, tea cost two shillings a pound but was taxed at five shillings a pound.

Huge profits offered irresistible temptation from the respectable aristocracy to the criminal underclass. By 1760 there were 800 items which had import duty paid on them. By 1810 this had mushroomed to 2,100 items. Every new tax made another item profitable for the smugglers. The smuggling industry reversed from exporting wool to importing these luxury items. France, Britain's bitter rival, built warehouses for British smugglers to stock up their orders. The goods pre-packaged, waterproofed and designed for being carried on packhorse and human shoulders.

To counter the rise in smuggling Parliament passed increasingly repressive measures. In 1698 the Revenue augmented their staff of Land, Coast and Tide Waiters with Riding Officers to patrol every part of the coast on horseback. In 1713 they were backed up by squadrons of dragoons, a type of mounted light infantry. The Revenue also employed ships, fast sloop-rigged "cutters", to intercept the smugglers at sea. Whole categories of vessels used in smuggling became illegal. Informants were paid £50 for betraying their comrades. Anyone found within five miles of the coast without good reason could be flogged or imprisoned. One could be hanged for simply dressing in disguise.

Despite these extreme laws the smuggling industry grew so fast that by the late Eighteenth Century the law had been almost completely subverted. In 1787 Prime Minister William Pitt estimated that 400,000 of the 600,000 gallons of brandy imported into Britain were smuggled. The trade was so profitable that it only needed one cargo in three getting through. Everyone benefited. The rich could acquire their luxuries, while poor labourers could earn in one night more than a week's pay on the land, plus some tea and brandy and a hot meal thrown in. The smugglers used a wide variety of vessels. The biggest were wide-beamed shallow draft 300 ton luggers. They could each carry 3,000 four-gallon keg barrels and twelve tons of tea and could cross the channel in just eight hours. They were armed with light cannon and manned by highly trained crews. In contrast the fourteen foot gigs of Bembridge also made a profitable trade with Cherbourg and Harfleur. Each could carry twenty tubs enough to finance "The building of many of the rows of Bembridge cottages".

The larger rowing galleys could be up to 120 feet in length with a beam of twenty feet. Unlike their pursuers they could row into the wind, and once beached, the rowers could carry the craft inland. A Revenue captain compared chasing a galley with a cutter to "sending a cow after a hare." All of Britain's intricate coastline was exploited by the smugglers but the main highway was across the Channel, particularly the coast from Hurst Castle to the Isle of Purbeck. The Island's location made

it an ideal storage depot "as if the Island were a huge smuggling lugger anchored just off the coast of the mainland" (Morley) The industry involved every section of society. It was led by the wealthy landed "Venturers" who organised the capital and facilitated the trade through their powerful positions in local society, for example as magistrates. Their bailiffs often doubled as "Agents" the gentlemen responsible for collecting in the shares from the farmers and wealthier people.

The Agents also accompanied the Captain of the smuggling ship to the great depots in the France and the Channel Islands to complete the order. The local clergyman or school teacher would become the "Clerk" who would secretly record the complex accounts. When the time came for a landing the bulk of the labouring population and farm animals were employed in moving the contraband inshore. "Tubmen" carried the tubs of brandy, guarded from attack by "Batmen", thugs armed with clubs, and later, despite the death penalty, with pistols. Once these "Gentlemen of the Night" had dispersed the cargo the detailed processing and distribution involved most of the rest of the population.

*Shanklin Chine was no doubt an important point of entry for smuggled goods like all Chines in the cliffs of the Island's south coast. A garrison of Revenue Officers was stationed in the Old Village. It was also popular with the Island's first tourists. In 1817 local longshoreman William Colenutt built the steps and started to charge for them, making this the Island's oldest commercial tourist attraction. Courtesy of Dr Robin McInnes OBE.*

"Practically all the houses on the East and West coasts of the Island were used as places of concealment". Houses were built with secret storage spaces incorporated in their design. Tubs were also hidden in haystacks, ploughed fields, tombs, disguised as chalk rocks, or dug into holes in gardens. The women watered down the 98 degree proof brandy and added the burnt sugar to provide the brown colour the British market expected. Then the contraband had to be dispersed, in ever smaller amounts, hidden in baskets and clothing to escape detection on the road. On the Island each village had its own gang and gang leader, who was probably the "Lander", the beachmaster controlling the movement of the contraband from ship to secret cache. As their power grew, the law became a joke.

The Revenue service was riddled with corruption and if its officers could not be bribed they were opposed with violence. For example in 1754 when two Riding Officers attempted to arrest Tim Dyer in the hamlet of Ventnor they were beaten up by his family and friends. Even in Cowes, where the Revenue head-quarters was based, the law was openly flouted. When William Goodwin raided the house of Thomas Francis the Constable refused him entry to a particular room until all the brandy within had been poured away. In 1770 when two officers arrested John Hall in the *Plume and Feathers* they were assaulted in the street and the liberated Hall fired a couple of pistols after them for good measure.

When William Arnold took up the Post of Collector of Customs at Cowes in 1777 he found the smugglers building their ships in the port and trading contraband to Hampshire in broad daylight. He felt powerless as the revenue cutters had been withdrawn for service in the American War of Independence (1775-1783). He reported to London that the smugglers were using big cutters and luggers of up to 300 tons, and so powerfully armed that the revenue men were powerless to stop them even in daylight. These ships escorted convoys of smaller vessels and were unloaded by gangs of up to three hundred men. Arnold appealed for not only cutters but also a warship to cope with the superior smuggling ships. At the end of the war the government provided him ships as his methods proved effective. The tipping point came with the deployment of *HMS Orestes* a 300 ton 18 gun sloop of war. In 1784 *Orestes* fought two battles capturing two heavily armed smuggling ships.

*The Island's militia on manoeuvres at Sandown Bay, showing Sandham Fort (left), by Richard Livesey. The Island was on the front line of the wars against Revolutionary and Napoleonic France which lasted a generation from 1793 to 1815. The Island was garrisoned with troops in various locations with a central barracks cut out of Parkhurst Forest in 1798, the site of the later prisons at Parkhurst and Albany. Courtesy of Dr Robin McInnes OBE.*

By the mid 1780s Arnold had control of the Solent and began to extend his power over the gangs on the Island and established regular intensive surveillance of whole coast. In 1785 this tough policy led to the shooting dead of Thomas Sivell of Binstead when the revenue boarded his ship in the Spithead. His gravestone records a great sense of injustice:-

*All you that pass pray look and see*
*How soon my life was took from me*
*They spill'd my blood that was so dear*
*But God is Good and just and true*
*And will reward to each their due*

Arnold died in 1801, an early death generally attributed to overwork. He was an exceptional civil servant in an age of universal corruption in public service. He is remembered now as the father of the famous Dr Thomas Arnold, later Master of Rugby, who appears in *Tom Brown's Schooldays,* who taught a new generation of Victorian civil servants his father's values.

The Golden Age of Smuggling came to an end after the final victory over France at Waterloo in 1815. The following year the Royal Navy took over the revenue cutters. The navy was well prepared by years of blockade of the continent and the impact was immediate. Seizures for 1816 included 875 smuggling vessels, 370,000 gallons of spirits, 42,000 yards of silk and 19,000lbs of tea.

The result of this clampdown was a new era of "Scientific Smuggling". This involved smaller cleverer operations, greater secrecy and guile. Contraband was now often hidden within legal goods such as hollowed and waterproofed hams. Parts of ships were built hollow, even down to the handles of oars being used to hide brandy. Tobacco was plaited into the hemp rigging and cargoes of contraband increasingly dragged underwater and dropped in shallows for retrieval later. In 1822 the Preventive Water Guard, established in 1809, was transformed into the Coastguard. Along the south coast they added 151 manned stations and 65 vessels to the forces of the Revenue and Navy. The Island landscape is dotted with their neat military terraces. Despite these measures the extent to which the Island was still ruled by free traders is well illustrated by the trial of Lieutenant Josiah Dornford in 1836 at Yarmouth.

Dornford commanded the Freshwater Coastguard and one night managed to miss a two hour gunfight when his colleagues at Totland were overwhelmed by a gang of smugglers. Two of the Totland Coastguards were badly beaten and Dornford was accused of collusion with the free traders. What is most telling about the trial is the fact that so many of the Island's gentry and clergy came to the trial to show their support for Dornford that his acquittal was assured.

Dornford's boss Commander Deare wrote to his superiors that year. Despite the fact that his men had arrested ten ships and eighty-one smugglers in the period 1834-36, he still felt it was a losing battle, "eight out of ten of the population are consumers of contraband... and they consider there is no harm in it." He noted that spirits on the Island were £1 cheaper per tub "less than in any part of the coast of Hampshire" which shows that the Island continued to act as an offshore wholesale depot for the south of England.

In the following years Parliament was increasingly divided on the issue of free trade. In 1846 the Tories split, many joining the liberal Whigs to repeal the Corn Laws and other restrictions to trade. In 1848 alone 450 items were liberated from liability to tax. Smuggling declined. As late as 1860 it was still the fulltime occupation of the men of Niton but in the 1870s the Niton gang were partly gaoled. After 1875 smuggling yarns were acquiring the stuff of legend. The code of secrecy ensured that most of the old protagonists took the true stories to their graves. As a result little is known as nothing was written down. We are just left with some stories and popular poems.

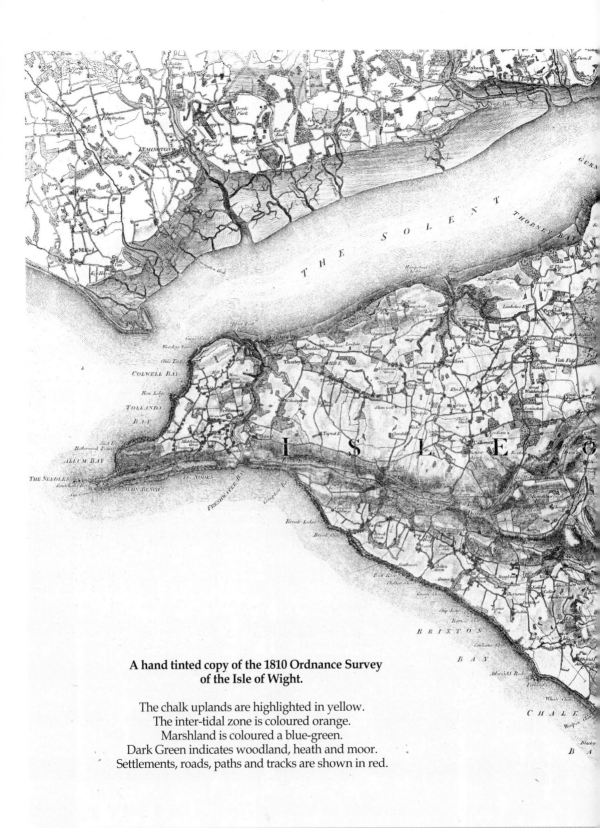

**A hand tinted copy of the 1810 Ordnance Survey
of the Isle of Wight.**

The chalk uplands are highlighted in yellow.
The inter-tidal zone is coloured orange.
Marshland is coloured a blue-green.
Dark Green indicates woodland, heath and moor.
Settlements, roads, paths and tracks are shown in red.

43

# THE HISTORY OF COWES & YACHTING

For over two centuries the Island port of Cowes has been at the centre of the world of yachting. The invention of the sport is credited to Charles II who Samuel Pepys records in his diary racing his yacht against his brother's in the River Thames in 1661. The Dutch word "yacht" came to be applied to any vessel used for cruising and racing. As the fashion for yachting grew among the high aristocracy from the 1660s to 1800s, the Solent area became one of the most advanced wooden ship and boat-building areas in the world as the Royal Navy, smugglers and the Customs men all ordered faster craft. The Solent itself not only offered highly skilled craftsmen and seamen but also offered yachtsmen an ideal place to race. The relatively sheltered waters made racing and regattas easier to run. The Solent is a unique piece of water characterised by double tides and changeable winds; excellent for challenging competitive racing.

*The first record of a regatta with naval cutters at Cowes, a painting by Dominic Serres made in 1776. Courtesy of the Royal Yacht Squadron.*

The first recorded regatta in Cowes was painted in 1776. Another was recorded in 1784 "a race of yachts of 24 tons with their racing flags in colour" The first round the Island race is recorded in 1788 for vessels under 35 tons for a prize of 30 guineas. The French wars of 1793-1815 attracted to Cowes "the complete spectrum of seafarers and those who lived by servicing their professional needs". At the same time the aristocracy deprived of their continental summer holidays found it "fashionable to take a house at Cowes." It is clear yachting practice was developing, by 1817 a vocabulary of 3,000 signals was in use. In 1812 the first official regatta took place at Cowes. The following year the crowds afloat and ashore were entertained by a parade of pilot cutters.

In June 1815, as the Napoleonic Wars finally ended at Waterloo, forty-two aristocrats, all of them owners of boats over 10 tons, gathered in the *Thatched House Tavern* in London to form "The Yacht club "...for those interested in salt-water sailing." They agreed that they would meet each August with their ships at Cowes. In 1817 the Prince Regent (after 1820 George IV) asked to become a member, soon followed by the Royal Dukes of Clarence and Gloucester. The Yacht Club became the Royal Yacht club in 1825, and finally the Royal Yacht Squadron in 1831 to recognise its intimate links to the Royal Navy.

The earliest club yachts varied from a converted Arab dhow to the 325 ton full rigged ship *Louisa*. With such diversity cruising was more important than racing. Yachts were heavily armed to fend off attack by pirates as they sailed to the Mediterranean and began to venture across the oceans. In 1830 the 58 ton cutter *Dolphin* was the first yacht to cross the Atlantic with a crew of four. In 1839 Sir James Brooke sailed a 142 ton schooner to Borneo where after a series of adventures he became Rajah of Sarawak in 1841.

Races between individual club members are recorded from 1815 onwards but group racing took longer to organise. In 1826 the Club organised its first recorded regatta. The first race began at 9.30am on Thursday 10th August for a "Gold Cup of the value of £100". Seven yachts competed in this first race. As a result of the success of this first race the people of Cowes offered two new cups, of 100 and 50 guineas. In the second gold cup race the previous winner *Arrow* became entangled with the *Miranda* resulting in hand to hand fighting between the crews. The regatta lasted three days including a ball and a firework display. The following year King George presented his own cup for the Cowes Regatta which grew into a four day racing event, always finished off with a firework display.

The regatta has been repeated in early August every year (except during the two World Wars) since 1826. This makes Cowes Week the longest running, regular regatta in the world. Offshore racing was being invented at the same time. In 1834 Lord Belfast's brig *Waterwitch* beat the *Galatea* in the first ocean yacht race from the Nab Tower to Eddystone Lighthouse. In 1846, at the time that the Squadron's first Commodore Lord Yarborough (1815-1846) died, the RYS had "become the unquestioned leader of yachting in the world." At this time there were sixteen royal yacht clubs. The RYS was easily the largest with 102 vessels totalling 900 tons and manned by 1,600 experienced seamen. In 1850 the RYS challenged the world to the £100 round the Island Royal Yacht Squadron Cup which was won by the veteran *Arrow*.

*Lord Craven's Louisa in company with HMS Wasp by Antoine Roux. Courtesy of the Royal Yacht Squadron.*

*The schooner America off Cowes in 1851 by T.S.Robins. Courtesy of The Royal Yacht Squadron.*

The following year the British yachting world was stunned by the arrival of the US schooner *America*. Her success in the 1851 race was to start a tradition of intense international competition. Her revolutionary design caused Lord Anglesey to remark, "If she's right, we must all be wrong." The *America* took the "America's" Cup home to New York Yacht Club where it remained, fiercely contested, until captured by the Australians in 1983. In 1858 the year the RYS moved into Henry VIII's Cowes Castle, the French Emperor Louis Napoleon initiated the first cross Channel races, according to increasingly complex "handicap" rules which were developed throughout the century to cope with the different tonnages and sail areas.

British royalty in the persons of Queen Victoria and the Prince Regent, resident at East Cowes from 1845, continued to increase the popularity of Cowes Week. In 1865 their son Edward; Prince of Wales became a member and took a keen interest in the sport. He had his first win in 205 ton *Hildegarde* in 1876. Prince Edward's participation in Cowes Week transformed it. Cowes was no longer, "a half civilised resort of the sailor man. It is now a court." In 1882 Edward was elected Commodore of the RYS. His commodorship coincided in a remarkable growth in the popularity of yacht racing. In 1889 his nephew the German Emperor William II began racing at Cowes which prompted Edward to build perhaps the greatest yacht of all time – *Britannia* in 1892.

The wood and steel cutter inspired the building of a series of similar yachts. In 1894 *Britannia* beat her American rival the *Satanita* 12 times in 17 races. In 1896 the Kaisers new 89 foot *Meteor* took on the 88 foot *Britannia* and won 13 races compared to *Britannia's* 11 wins. Disillusioned, Prince Edward sold *Britannia* and retired from competitive racing. From this time yachting began to change type and size. 1896 saw the beginning of the small eight ton Solent One design class, uniform sized boats that would symbolise modern inshore yacht racing. Ocean racing also became more popular. The Kaiser initiated the annual Dover-Heligoland cup in 1897 and the greatest race of the period, the 1905 transatlantic Kaisers Cup of 1905 from New York to Cowes, which was repeated by Rolex in 1997 and in 2005.

Petrol-driven speedboat racing also became increasingly popular, championed by Lord Montague of Beaulieu and Lionel de Rothschild. The American *Dixie* won the British International trophy in 1907 but *Maple Leaf* won it back in 1912 and defended it successfully in Osborne bay in 1913. Squadron members continued to cruise more than race. In 1876-77 RYS member Lord Brassey achieved the first circumnavigation of the Earth by a yacht in the *Sunbeam*. Another world sailor was Frank James who was killed by an elephant he shot in West Africa in 1890. His brothers built the Frank James hospital in East Cowes in his memory. By the outbreak of war 1914 the RYS had 246 members. A French count described it in 1899 as "the most select club, the most aristocratic, the most closed, and the most intransigent, not just in England but in the whole world."

The 1914-18 war broke out just as the regatta was about to begin. The Squadron's yachts became part of the navy as inshore patrol boats. Cowes Castle became a home for convalescent naval affairs. The war put paid to yachting for five years. There was still no regatta in 1919. 1920 the regatta was restored when George V had *Britannia* prepared for racing. Others quickly followed suit. This began the great inter-war period of yachting. The "J Class" raced until the 1930's but the real interest continued to be in the smaller international classes, such as the Solent One Design races. In 1923 the 19m *Paula III* beat *Britannia* in a combined race, signifying the rise of smaller yachts. *Britannia* continued to race to 1935. Following the death of King George V she was scuppered in St. Catherine's Deep in line with his wish. Between 1893 and 1935 she had taken part in 565 races and had come first in 231.

The prestigious British-American Cup was raced alternately each year at Cowes and New York from 1921 until 1940. The bi-annual Fastnet Race began in 1925 and British victory led to the formation of the Royal Ocean Racing Club in 1931. The first Santander race was organised in 1929. Power Boat and small yacht class races continued to proliferate. The Prince of Wales Cup for fourteen foot dinghies was won a record twelve times by Cowes based Stewart Morris.

*Osborne House by George Brannon in the 1820's before it was acquired by Queen Victoria and Prince Albert in 1845.*
*Courtesy of the Isle of Wight Records Office.*

During the Second World War (1939-1945) the RYS became *HMS Vectis*. From 1946 the world of yachting began to change. The large cruising yachts became a thing of the past along with the large classes of inshore racers. Ocean racing became the competitive domain of the large yachts while smaller boats continued to be increasingly popular. The first Admiral's Cup was sailed for in 1957 and the two ocean races that start and finish the week - the Channel and Fastnet races - began to gain in popularity. After World War II yachting changed from being the province of the rich to a sport for the enthusiast. Another generation of young royals, Princess Elizabeth and the Duke of Edinburgh joined the RYS in 1948. The Duke raced enthusiastically and won a number of races. In 1961 he was invited to become the eleventh Commodore of the Squadron. He accepted but on conditions. From now on the post would be for six years, not for life, two Vice Commodores were appointed and a breeze of change could be sensed.

Prince Phillip's most important contribution was in the reorganisation of Cowes Week. Up to 1963 the weeks events were organised by different clubs on different days, with different start lines and different rules. From 1964 to this day Cowes Week is run by Cowes Combined Clubs (CCC) with all races starting at the same start lines according to rules agreed between all the clubs. The clubs are the RYS, the Royal Thames, (founded in 1775 and present at Cowes from 1953) the Royal Southern (1844) Royal Southampton (1866) Cowes Town Regatta Committee, active since 1869, the Royal London, which relocated to Cowes in 1882, The Royal Corinthian (1872) the Island Sailing Club (1889) East Cowes Sailing Club (1912) and the Royal Ocean Racing Club (1925).

Other notable yachtsmen who made a big impact in the postwar expansion of the sport were Max Aitken, the designer Uffa Fox, Sir Francis Chichester and Sir Edward Heath. The former Prime Minister won sixteen ocean races of fifty-four and captained the team that won back the Admirals Cup from the Americans. Sir Francis Chichester organised and won the first Single-Handed Transatlantic Race in 1960. In 1967 he won the first solo circumnavigation of the Earth which led to the current Volvo Ocean Race. Max Aitken was a prolific yachtsman and powerboat racer. His former home in Cowes High Street is now a fascinating nautical museum. Cowes Week now has over forty racing classes; the number of boats taking part is around 1,000. Classes include cruiser-racers, one designs and keelboat classes. The activities ashore are just as much part of the whole event. They vary from cocktail parties, yacht club balls, private parties and public events at Northwood House, including the spectacular fireworks display held on the final Friday evening, which is attended by tens of thousands of people both watching from the shore and from hundreds of yachts which gather around the harbour.

However Cowes Week is just the climax. Over the whole of 2000 for example an estimated thirty-three thousand yachts and two hundred thousand yachtsmen visited Cowes along with a half million onlookers. Some one fifth of the Island's tourist income comes from yachting. The Round the Island race is the largest and most popular yacht race in the world. Two thousand vessels take part. Perhaps the most stunning display in recent years was the 150th anniversary of the America's Cup. Over 200 yachts averaging 72 feet long took part in six days of racing including all the surviving J Class and 37 12 metre class, square riggers and modern racers like the 250 foot *Leander*.

*West Cowes as seen by Queen Victoria on her visits to Osborne House.*
*Courtesy of Dr Robin McInnes OBE.*

# ISLAND OF GENIUS 1800-1901

After reading a detailed account of the Battle of Balaklava (1854) the Poet Laureate Alfred Tennyson took his daily walk from Farringford House in Freshwater up onto the High Down. As he strode forward in hat and cape his thoughts concentrated on one incident of the battle. Lines of poetry rumbled through his mind to the rhythm of cantering cavalry; "half a league, half a league, half a league onward, into the valley of death rode the six hundred, guns to the right of them, guns to the left of them, guns to the front of them volleyed and thundered... not though the soldier knew, someone had blundered". He returned home to write one of the most famous poems in the English language, "*The Charge of the Light Brigade*".

*Orchard Cottage on the Undercliff is typical of the many stylish retreats built by wealthy Overners in the Nineteenth Century. They were built in particular along the coastline between Cowes and St Helens, Sandown and Chale in order to benefit from the striking sea views. Their design was often "romantic" and "gothic" to fit in with the Island's picturesque countryside. Courtesy of Dr Robin McInnes OBE.*

During the Nineteenth Century the Isle of Wight became known as a focus of intellectual genius. Tennyson is best remembered for his celebrated status as Britain's greatest poet and his permanent residence in Freshwater for almost forty years. Many other great men, poets, writers, artists, architects, philosophers, statesmen, theologians and pioneers of science all came to the Island.

## *An Artists Paradise*

The notoriety of the Island as a bucolic idyll reminiscent of a fast disappearing rural England was well established by 1800, thanks to artists such as Thomas Rowlandson and Samuel Jowett. The greatest British landscape painter of the century, Joseph Mallord William Turner (1774-1851) visited several times and painted the Needles and Carisbrooke Castle. In the early part of the century Cowes Week developed under the patronage of kings George IV (1820-1830) and William IV 1830–1837). Cowes attracted many great marine artists and other famous visitors along with the sailing aristocracy. Of all the talented architects who worked on the Island the greatest must be John Nash. He built himself the magnificent Gothic style East Cowes Castle. Nash had already

*Freshwater resident Alfred Lord Tennyson photographed by Julia Margaret Cameron. He was the Poet Laureate from 1850 to his death in 1892.*
*Courtesy of the Julia Margaret Cameron Trust.*

designed Brighton Pavilion, Buckingham Palace and much of the iconic landscape of Westminster. He also designed Newport's Guildhall. From 1846 the presence of the Royal Family guaranteed the Island's notoriety and popularity with the intelligentsia of Victorian Britain. They concentrated in particular on Carisbrooke Castle, then an overgrown romantic ruin, the spectacular Undercliff between Shanklin and Blackgang and the dramatic cliffs of Freshwater Bay. The families of the longshoremen who eked a living from these coasts, and their humble stone and thatch cottages were repeatedly painted and their likenesses exhibited in the Royal Academy.

In *"Isle of Wight Illustrated"* Dr Robin McInnes identified 276 major artists and engravers who are known to have published or exhibited views of the Island between 1770 and 1915. The light and fresh nature of the Island seemed a world away form the soot-blackened towns of industrial Britain where most Britons lived by 1851. As a result these Island views were enormously popular as a form of public escapism.

## Writers and Poets

Others found the Island a good place to think. One of the greatest of the Romantic poets, John Keats (1795-1821) began perhaps his most famous poem, *Endymion,* at Carisbrooke in 1819. The opening lines are redolent of balmy Island summer days:-

> *"A thing of beauty is a joy forever*
> *Its loveliness increases; it will never*
> *Pass into nothingness; but still will keep*
> *A bower quiet for us, and a sleep*
> *Full of sweet dreams, and health, and quiet breathing"*

Already terminally ill, Keats spent the summer of 1819 on the Island, mostly at Shanklin, at Eglantine Cottage where the artist George Morland and the dramatist Thomas Morton had stayed in previous years.

In 1868 the great American poet Henry Wadsworth Longfellow (1807-1882) was also captivated by Shanklin. He stayed at the "lovely little thatch-roof" Crab Inn "all covered in ivy and extremely desirable... it is all like a scene on a stage... when the chambermaid appears you expect she will sing instead of speak". Further south and still more remote from Shanklin the tiny village of Bonchurch later attracted a whole colony of artists and thinkers. The Swinburnes bought East Dene in 1839. This wild countryside was where the future Pre-Raphaelite poet Algernon Swinburne fell in love with the cliffs and the sea. William Sewell of the Oxford Movement and his talented family arrived in 1844. In 1849 Charles Dickens (1812-1870) the greatest of all the Victorian novelists stayed over the road from the Sewells at Winterbourne. He was writing *David Copperfield,* but still found time for a prize giving for the new school, giving conjuring performances and in games of rounders with other literary lights on the beach at Monks Bay.

At Christmas 1854 Swinburne decided to prove his courage by walking and swimming Sandown Bay to climb Culver Cliff. He was defeated in his first attempt by an overhanging ledge and on his second climb his footing gave way leaving him swinging in the air, hanging by his fingers. When he finally ascended onto the top of Culver Down, he fell unconscious. He awoke to the close stare of a concerned sheep which he terrified away with his laughter. Like Tennyson, Swinburne wrote some of his greatest works in the 1860s, in particular *Atalanta in Calydon* published in 1864. The following year his father sold East Dene but when Swinburne died in 1909 this "last of the great Victorians" was buried in the graveyard at St Boniface church. His poems include beautiful imagery directly taken from his years at Bonchurch, Brook and Shorwell.

The outstanding female author of the period George Eliot (1819-1880) who wrote *Middlemarch* and *Silas Marner* among others visited the Island several times. In 1863 she stayed in Niton Post Office enjoying the home made bread, cream and butter for 25 shillings a week (£1.25) which included a servant in a crinoline dress.

*Charles Darwin who stayed at Freshwater after publishing Origin of the Species in 1859 which established the theory of evolution.*

## The Tennysons at Farringford

Alfred and Emily Tennyson first came to live in the Farringford estate in 1853. In 1850 he had been made Poet Laureate on the death of Wordsworth, the last of the great romantic poets. Unlike the romantics Tennyson was deeply interested in the moral problems of his time. His range of contemporary interests is indicated in the people he invited to stay at Farringford. Many returned to stay in other houses in nearby Freshwater Bay or to buy and build their own properties.

In 1860 he invited Charles Darwin (1809-1882), the greatest scientist of the century who stayed at Redoubt House in Freshwater Bay. Tennyson recognised that *Origin of the Species*, published in 1859 did not undermine Christianity as the fundamentalists claimed. Darwin brought his horse when he came to stay and rode it on the downs. In 1864 Tennyson invited the Italian nationalist revolutionary Guiseppe Garibaldi. Three years earlier Garibaldi had led a thousand red-shirted volunteers into the invasion and revolutionary overthrow of the Bourbon Kingdom of Naples and Sicily leading to the unification of Italy.

*Julia Margaret Cameron, photography pioneer and resident of Freshwater, 1860-1875.*
*Courtesy of*
*The Julia Margaret Cameron Trust*

While in Freshwater Garibaldi was accosted by a woman begging on her knees. It was non other than Julia Margaret Cameron (1815-1879) desperate to get the old man to sit for a photograph. The previous year this amazing pioneer had converted a coal-shed and chicken house into dark room and studio to work with the smelly difficult new technology of photography. "I worked fruitlessly but not hopelessly." Then she started to get startling results. She was inventing a new artform. "I longed to arrest all the beauty that came across my way." In a short but brilliant career she won gold silver and bronze medals in Britain, the USA, Austria Hungary and Germany. She photographed the historian Thomas Carlyle, Trollope the novelist, a future archbishop the artist G.F. Watts, the scientist Sir John Herschell and many others.

# The "Freshwater Set"

The Cameron's home at Dimbola (1860) became a sort of central social club for the artistic society developing in Freshwater as Julia organized theatricals, concerts and dances that spilled onto the lawns. Freshwater must have become a duller place when in 1875 the Camerons packed their coffins to return to their tea estates in Sri Lanka. Something of the spirit of the time was caught in Virginia Woolf's play *Freshwater*, based on her own memories. One visitor was heard to exclaim "Is there no-one who is commonplace here? Is everybody either a poet, or a genius, or a painter or peculiar in some way?"

George Watts the artist built the Briary and the sculptor Thomas Woolner worked at Farringford. Among other Freshwater visitors and characters are the author of *Vanity Fair* William Makepeace Thackeray, the inventor of the limerick, Edward Lear, thinker John Ruskin and poet Robert Browning. Both Lewis Carroll and his inspiration for *Alice in Wonderland*, Alice Liddel, were visitors. She was photographed several times by Cameron.

Between the deaths of Tennyson in 1892 and Queen Victoria in 1901 another genius, the young Guglielmo Marconi transmitted radio signals to ships at sea from his laboratory at the Royal Needles Hotel, opening a new era of electronic mass communication. Thus ended the era of memorized poetry recitals as surely as the camera replaced paint and canvass in the new era of popular culture.

Into the Twentieth Century the Island remained popular with artists and writers and thinkers. Freshwater Bay alone can boast Kipling, George Bernard Shaw, W.H. Auden, Christopher Isherwood, J.B. Priestley and John Betjeman as later visitors.

*Scientist Sir John Herschell by Cameron. He originally inspired her to the new science and left us with the words "photograph" "negative" and "snapshot". Courtesy of the Isle of Wight Council.*

*Sir John Simeon, resident of Swainston, one of Tennyson's closest friends, in a bust made by Thomas Woolner. It was recently discovered on a shelf in Calbourne Mill. Courtesy of Elizabeth Hutchings.*

# THE PRINCESS OF THE WIGHT

*Princess Beatrice painted in 1928 by Arthur Stockdale Cope.*
*Courtesy of Carisbrooke Castle Museum.*

2007 marks the 150th anniversary of the birth of the Island's unique resident royal, Princess Beatrice, the youngest daughter of Queen Victoria. The event was marked by an exhibition in the Carisbrooke Castle Museum which she founded in 1898. Princess Beatrice lived most of her long life from 1857 to 1944 on the Island, either at Osborne House or later later at Carisbrooke Castle. She once gloriously married and now lies entombed with her husband in Whippingham Church. On the 14th of April 1857 cannon roared from the walls of the Tower of London to announce the birth at Buckingham Palace of the ninth and last child of Queen Victoria and Prince Albert.

Beatrice was born into the most fabulous court in the world, the symbolic centre of the world's greatest empire. She was brought up largely at Osborne where her parents had designed a perfect modern education. She learned to ride and swim, studied nature, gardening and household management in the Swiss Cottage in the palace grounds. She learned to paint, the skills of needlework, and to compose music.

In 1861 when Beatrice was just four years old her adoring father died of typhoid. Victoria changed overnight from a confident spirited mother into a grieving recluse. Osborne changed from being a happy family home into a sort of mausoleum where Albert's things remained untouched. For the last forty years of her reign Victoria was in a permanent state of mourning and Beatrice her constant companion. Between 1857 and 1882 all of Beatrice's older brothers and sisters married. In 1882 Beatrice was 25 years old, left living alone with her grieving mother. Victoria needed Beatrice as a personal companion.

## Beatrice & Henry

Beatrice knew and accepted her duty but in 1884, on a trip to Germany she met and fell in love with the dashing Prince Henry Maurice of Battenburg who was a year her junior. Prince Henry proposed and Beatrice accepted. Victoria was concerned that she would lose her daughter but Henry agreed to come and live at Osborne. The wedding that took place at Whippingham Church in 1885 was the greatest royal occasion that the Island ever witnessed.

200 guests from London, including the ambassadors and politicians were brought by special train to take their seats at the church. Prince Henry, wearing the white uniform of a captain of the Prussian Cuirassiers, arrived at East Cowes to a roar of cannon and an ecstatic public welcome. The streets from East Cowes to the church were lined by the Argyll and Sutherland Highlanders in crimson tunics and tartan kilts.

A procession of fourteen carriages left Osborne House. The royal route was decorated with flags hung on masts, triumphal arches and stands for the crowds to get a view. A boarded footway and canopy led from the churchyard gate to the church door, with additional seating built outside. Inside the church the floor had been covered in crimson cloth and oriental rugs. "exquisite flowers were everywhere" reported The Illustrated London News.

Just eight Islanders made it into the church for this state occasion. In place of the vicar were the Lord Chamberlain, the Archbishop of Canterbury, the Bishop of Winchester and the Dean of Windsor. In place of the local choir was the choir of St George's Chapel, Windsor. The royal family took their seats to the sound of Handel's March from the Occasional Overture.

Then, at 1pm, the Wedding March sounded and Princess Beatrice advanced along the aisle accompanied by ten royal brides maids dressed in ivory gowns. Beatrice wore a beautiful dress of white satin trimmed with lace, decorated with orange blossom, myrtle and heather; her veil emblazoned with diamonds. With the service complete the wedding party returned to Osborne through the cheering crowds. Two large boarded reception marquees had been built either side of the palace. One was reserved for the guests of "royal blood" and the other was for the rest. Back at the church there was no such decorum. The excited crowds rushed in to seize any momentos of the great occasion.

*Princess Beatrice photographed on the day of her spectacular wedding at Whippingham Church.*
*Courtesy of the Isle of Wight Records Office.*

Beatrice and Henry settled to happy married life at Osborne. Over the next five years she gave birth to Alexander, Victoria Eugenie, Leopold and Maurice. Prince Henry became the Honorary Colonel of the local territorial regiment, the IW Rifles, a job he took seriously. Items of his uniform and the fine sword he presented the regiment can be seen in Carisbrooke Castle Museum. In 1889 he became Governor and Captain of the Island, but the problem for Henry was that these were now largely ceremonial roles. The soldier in him yearned for action and he finally received a posting to fight in the Fourth Ashanti War (1894-1896) in modern Ghana. In January 1896 Henry died of malaria and in February he was interred at Whippingham Church where he had married just ten years before.

## *The Princess Becomes Governor*

The widowed Beatrice, now 38 years old, did not retreat into seclusion like her mother. In 1897 she took over her husbands offices of Governor of the Isle of Wight and Captain and also supported a concert to raise funds for the relief of a famine in India. In 1898 she opened a memorial museum to Henry in the gate house at Carisbrooke Castle. It is from this small beginning that the Island's museums and archaeological services were to evolve. After her mother died at Osborne in 1901 Beatrice's life at the centre of court life ended. Her brother "Bertie", the new King Edward VII (1901-1910) closed Osborne. Beatrice was left with Osborne and Albert cottages off York Avenue in East Cowes.

Governess Beatrice took an active part in Island life, supporting the great pageant of Island History at Carisbrooke Castle in 1907. In 1911, on the succession of "my dear nephew King George V" she issued all the Island's schoolchildren with coronation medals. In 1913 the Governor's rooms at Carisbrooke Castle became vacant. Beatrice decided to take up her right to residence, sold her property in East Cowes and moved in after making some alterations, such as adding a bathroom, as life at the castle remained rather primitive.

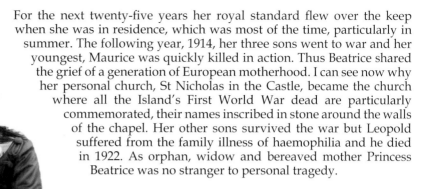

For the next twenty-five years her royal standard flew over the keep when she was in residence, which was most of the time, particularly in summer. The following year, 1914, her three sons went to war and her youngest, Maurice was quickly killed in action. Thus Beatrice shared the grief of a generation of European motherhood. I can see now why her personal church, St Nicholas in the Castle, became the church where all the Island's First World War dead are particularly commemorated, their names inscribed in stone around the walls of the chapel. Her other sons survived the war but Leopold suffered from the family illness of haemophilia and he died in 1922. As orphan, widow and bereaved mother Princess Beatrice was no stranger to personal tragedy.

The period that Beatrice lived at Carisbrooke (1913-1938) is still remembered by some living Islanders. According to Kathleen Pritchard "She always attended St Mary's (Carisbrooke) church for matins on Sunday mornings. As she and her lady in waiting entered the church the congregation stood and sang the national anthem. During the final hymn the Sunday School children would leave the church and wait in the porch for her to emerge. We usually had small bunches of flowers to give which we had picked in Priory Fields" (now Carisbrooke Park Estate). "Her Royal Highness always spent time talking to us and the rest of the congregation and when it was time for her to leave from the lych gate we children would run and wave her off and she in turn would wave and call out "Goodbye children, see you next week".

*Prince Henry of Battenburg dressed in the uniform of the Island's Territorial regiment, the Isle of Wight Rifles of which he was Colonel. Courtesy of Carisbrooke Castle Museum.*

Beatrice gave the church an antique processional cross and supported the fundraising for the church hall and a school room. She also supported the local scouts and guides, nursing organisations, art and needlework guilds. She gave her own paintings as prizes in local fetes. On her 80th birthday in 1937 the Islanders reciprocated with gifts including a 1603 chamber organ. The following summer was the last one she spent at Carisbrooke. After that she was taken care of on the Mainland. She died on a country estate on October 26th 1944.

## Beatrice's Final Wishes

Following the end of the Second World War in August 1945 Princess Beatrice's final wishes were granted. In bright September sunshine her coffin was carried by three motor torpedo boats through the fleet at Portsmouth and the Spithead. Four bluejackets stood at each corner of the coffin, rifles reversed, heads down. As the little flotilla passed, the ships companies of the Royal Navy paraded on their decks beneath half raised colours. The last of Queen Victoria's children was heading home. The coffin arrived at East Cowes for a very private service at Whippingham church. Only her son Alexander and his wife were present. At the end of the service he stepped forward to sprinkle lavender, picked from the garden of Gethsemane, onto his mother's coffin next to that of her husband Henry. Then the tomb was sealed with the inscription "Till death us do join".

Alexander Marquess of Carisbrooke was interred with his parents in 1960. As he had no son, his title died with him. However, through her daughter Victoria Eugenie, Beatrice's great grandson Juan Carlos restored the Spanish monarchy in 1975. The locations of Beatrice's turbulent life are all preserved, the active royal palaces, the conserved museum of Osborne. The current Carisbrooke Castle Museum is in the very rooms where Beatrice once lived.

# THE ISLE OF WIGHT STEAM RAILWAYS

In 1952 the Isle of Wight had a steam powered rail network of 55 miles linking places as far apart as Freshwater, Bembridge, St Lawrence and Cowes. This extraordinary system was built with the primitive but lasting engineering techniques of the mid-late nineteenth century. Despite the popularity of the system with its Victorian tank engines pulling trains through some of the most stunning scenery in the country, the system was closed down in the 1950s and 1960s. Only a fraction of the line, from Shanklin to Ryde, survived, now electrified and served with 1930s London tube trains. However, a number of people, appalled at the destruction of the steam railway were determined on saving just a tiny part of it. Thanks to their dedication, from 1971, the task of reconstruction and preservation at Havenstreet Station was begun. The Isle of Wight Steam Railway has now restored almost one tenth of the original steam powered network.

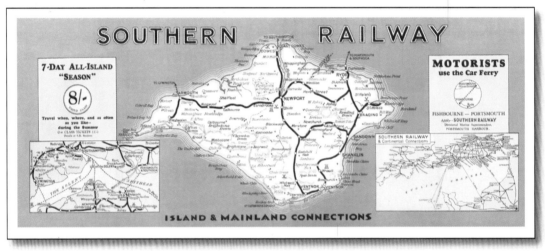

*In 1923 all the Island's railways were grouped together under Southern Railways.*
*This map of the time shows the complete Isle of Wight network.*
*Courtesy of the Isle of Wight Steam Railway.*

Railways were invented in Britain to move coal and later passengers and other goods in the industrial areas. By the 1830s inter-city railways began to thread across the country. In 1840 Southampton was connected to London by rail, and in 1842, Gosport. By the 1850s, even Islanders were considering the benefits of the speed of steam and the effect of falling transport costs. In 1859 an Act of Parliament was passed for a four and a half mile railway to be built between Cowes and Newport. Since 1770 the Cowes to Newport route had been serviced by a steel-spring stage-coach service from the Fountain Inn at Cowes to the Sun Inn at Newport. The coach made the journey there and back twice a day.

According to the *I.W. Observer* "the first sod was unostentatiously dug on October 16th 1859." After a long labour the railway was finally completed by the Cowes & Newport Railway Company and approved by government inspectors. It featured a tunnel near Mill Hill Station and part crossed the Medina Estuary on a wooden viaduct. It opened on the 16th of June 1862. The first train left Cowes at 08.15 and arrived in Newport less than ten minutes later, a journey time equivalent to the stoppage time for the stage coach. By the time the first passengers arrived back at Cowes, half an hour after leaving, they found their breakfast things had not yet even been cleared away. Over that first day an estimated 600-700 passengers travelled on the new train, the engine decorated in "laurels and evergreens, with pennants and flags on either side".

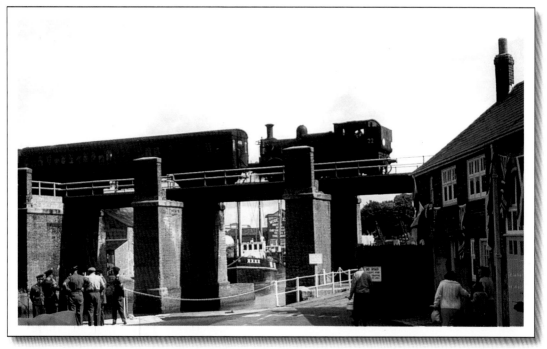

*The No 22 Brading crossing the Medina drawbridge in 1965. This was later replaced by the bridge of the dual carriageway Newport bypass. Newport Railway Station was just north of the town where the bypass now lies. Photo published in Andrew Britton's book Ryde by Steam. Courtesy of Isle of Wight Steam Railway.*

On August 23rd 1864 another company, the Isle of Wight Railway Company, opened a longer seven and a quarter miles line from Ryde St Johns Road to Shanklin. This was extended to Ventnor in 1866. The other stations on this line were Brading, Sandown and Wroxall. This line had the greatest challenge on the whole of the final Island network, a five and a half mile constant uphill climb from sea-level at Yaverland to the height of the Ventnor Tunnel 300ft above the sea.

The next line to be built was the Ryde & Newport Railway, which was sanctioned in 1872 and opened in December 1875. It was administered by the Cowes & Newport Railway, before the amalgamation in 1887, that formed the Isle of Wight Central Railway. The stations were Newport, ("Royal") Whippingham, Wootton, Havenstreet and Ashey. Smallbrook Junction joined the existing line to its final station at Ryde St. Johns Road.

The new system was extended with the construction of the ten mile Sandown to Newport line, planned by the Isle of Wight (Newport Junction) Railway company in 1868. The new railway failed to pass several safety inspections until it finally opened in 1879. From Newport, heading southeast, were the stations of Shide, Blackwater, Merstone, Horringford, Newchurch, Alverstone and finally Sandown. In 1880 the company fell into receivership. It was bought by the Isle of Wight Central Railway.

The main problem of the 1870s was that the Isle of Wight lines did not have a direct connection with the main ferries. In 1812 the original Ryde Pier had been constructed, and the main ferry to Portsmouth ran from there. A horse-drawn tram system linked Ryde Pier Head to Ryde St. Johns Road station, but this was unsatisfactory. Two Mainland companies, the London & South Western Railway and the London, Brighton & South Coast Railway, eager to get involved with the profitable trade on the Island, jointly constructed a railway line carried on the new half-mile long pier out to sea which they had constructed. The line continued inland, through a 391 yard tunnel down a steep gradient below sea level after Ryde Esplanade station, emerging just before coming into Ryde St. Johns Road. This was opened in July 1880.

In 1882, a new stretch of line from Brading to Bembridge was opened, with a third station in between at the village of St. Helens. This was run by the Isle of Wight Railway Company. A train ferry operated from here for six years, but closed in 1888. The next line to be opened on the Island carried passengers to the western towns of Yarmouth and Freshwater. The Freshwater, Yarmouth & Newport Railway was almost twelve miles long and opened in December 1890. It stopped at Freshwater, Yarmouth, Ningwood, Calbourne & Shalfleet, Watchingwell, Carisbrooke and finally Newport.

The final section of railway line to be opened on the Island was the Newport - Ventnor railway, part of the Isle of Wight Central Railway network. It ran from the junction at Merstone and headed south to Godshill, Whitwell and St. Lawrence, and was opened in July 1897 when it was described as "one of the prettiest branch lines in England". It was extended to Ventnor West station in June 1900. The network had now reached its greatest extent, supplemented and complemented by horse-drawn coaches and motor vehicle trips to places such as Alum Bay, Blackgang Chine, Appledurcombe, Brighstone, and other points of popular interest. Meanwhile rail investors considered their most ambitious project yet. The South Western and Isle of Wight Junction Railway planned to dig a two and a half mile tunnel under the western Solent to link the Lymington and Freshwater lines. The Solent Tunnel Project was approved by Parliament in the 1903, 1904 and 1909 sessions, but abandoned during the First World War, 1914-18.

During the war the railways were run by the government. In the succeeding decades there was very little investment in the system. The rise of motor traffic put the railways on the defensive. After 1923, the Island's railways were grouped together under the ownership of Southern Railway.

## What was the system like? How good was it?

According to Bradshaws British Railways Official Guide for 30th June to August 4th 1952, the last summer of the whole network, passengers on the Saturday 06.41 from London Victoria would arrive at 10.15 at Ryde Pier Head to go either south on the 10.25, or west on the 10.35. Both trains would stop at St Johns Road before the railway divided at Smallbrook Junction. The Newport train would arrive in Newport at 11.07 and passengers would either change for Cowes where the train would arrive at 11.19 or continue west to arrive in Freshwater at 11.53. The Ventnor train would steam out of the Island's longest tunnel under Boniface Down into Ventnor Station at 11.12.

So in the age of steam-powered trains and steamers London Victoria and Ventnor were under six hours apart. The equivalent journey from London Waterloo to Ventnor took just three hours and twenty-two minutes 07.50-11.12. In the other direction the 06.30 from Ventnor provided a comfortable 09.51 arrival at Waterloo, three hours and twenty-one minutes later. The frequency of the summer service was also remarkable. On Sundays 18 trains travelled from Ryde to Ventnor alone. Apart from a mail train that ran from 03.20 from the Pier Head to arrive at Ventnor at 04.53, the Ryde trains started meeting the steam ferries at 06.30. The Ryde trains rumbled down the pier about once an hour until the 21.40 to Ventnor. In the opposite direction trains set off from Cowes at 06.37, and Ventnor at 06.30 for the 07.30 half hour ferry ride from Ryde, to arrive at Victoria at 10.26. The last train to leave Yarmouth was at 20.10 for the 21.35 ferry.

In summer some parts of the system were very busy. Up to twelve trains per hour used Smallbrook Junction. Other routes were quieter. Nevertheless eleven trains left Freshwater for Newport every weekday and eight on Sundays. This was just one picturesque route, alongside the marshes of the Yar Estuary to Yarmouth Station (still intact) and over the fields and cross country to Carisbrooke Halt, finally entering Newport on an elevated bridge. Twenty-six trains left Bembridge Station on weekdays, circling the harbour to St Helens and on to meet the main line at Brading.

Fifteen trains set out from Cowes every weekday from 06.56 to 20.36 on a journey of an hour and forty minutes to Ventnor. From Newport Shide and Blackwater some went straight south from Merstone Junction to Godshill, Whitwell, St Lawrence and Ventnor West. Others went eastward

*The last day of steam on Ryde Pier, 17th September 1966.*
*Photo published in Ryde by Steam by Andrew Britton. Courtesy of Isle of Wight Steam Railway.*

beneath the downs to Horringford, Newchurch and Alverstone before joining the Ryde Ventnor line at Sandown. Considering that these old trains rattled along at a sedate safe speed, the journey times on the Island were remarkable. Currently a modern bus leaving Ryde station at 10.10 arrives at Ventnor station at 11.25, taking one and a quarter hours. The 10.25 steam train, with six compulsory stops, took three quarters of an hour, half an hour less than the modern bus.

The Victorian locomotives employed on the Island were all named after towns and villages on the Island. The Isle of Wight became a very popular tourist resort, especially the south-east coast towns of Sandown, Shanklin and Ventnor. During the Second World War (1939-1945) the railways were again run by the government and in 1948 were nationalised as British Rail. During the 1950s British Rail began the closure of rural branch lines throughout the UK, including here on the Island.

## *The Closure of the System*

The Ventnor West to Merstone line was the first to close in 1952. The Newport to Freshwater and the Brading to Bembridge lines closed the following year. The Sandown - Newport line closed in 1956, and despite much protest, the Ryde to Cowes line was closed in 1966, along with the Shanklin-Ventnor section of the Ryde - Ventnor line. The last passenger steam train service ran on December 31st 1966. The abandoned network was broken up very quickly.

The last of the old engines, No.24 *Calbourne*, was used in the electrification of the line from Ryde to Sandown and then passed into the hands of the Wight Locomotive Society. The society represented the steam rail enthusiasts who simply refused to accept this industrial vandalism. They modestly hoped to keep one locomotive and a few carriages as a static display. They were determined but few, and faced a wall of official hostility from the residual rail authorities. The Society saved just *Calbourne* of the dozen pre-1923 locomotives and five of the 50 historic carriages.

In 1969 *Calbourne* was at St John's Rd with a collection of five carriages and some wagons at the derelict station in Newport. As the line was already severed there was no way of getting *Calbourne* back to Newport until one of the society members "stumbled across a vast ginormous transporter" (Marion Hunnisett) and persuaded the crew in a nearby pub that the society could afford to hire them before they returned to the mainland. *Calbourne* was brought tortuously into Newport on August 15th, being finally heaved into the station by a tractor "and a vast crowd". In 1970 the County Council finally secured the line from Cowes to Ryde and set aside one and three quarter miles of track from Wootton to Havenstreet for the Society.

In January 1971 the scrap merchants gave the enthusiasts just four days to evacuate the decaying Newport Station. There had been a landslip at Fairlee, and the abandoned line was becoming unstable. In four perilous trips *Calbourne* pulled the six carriages and assorted trucks to safety at Havenstreet. Later that year *Calbourne* was joined by *Invincible* and work began on the restoration of the abandoned station and the overgrown line. One third of the wooden sleepers had to be replaced. It was just the beginning of untold tens of thousands of hours of work that would eventually lead to the establishment of one of the finest vintage railway museums in the country. It took over a decade to build a new Wootton Station.

In 1991 the line made a major expansion east to rebuild Ashey Halt and open a new station at Smallbrook Junction which now became the exchange junction for passengers onto the electrified Islandline. The railway now owned three of the original engines with the return to the Island of the *Newport* and *Freshwater*.

"All our carriages and most of our locomotives have spent much of their working lives here on the Island. They have all been painstakingly restored to pristine condition and are the hallmark of our delightful railway. Our oldest locomotive was built in 1876 and carriages date back to 1864." (promotional literature). The Isle of Wight Steam Railway is unique in the country through "an authentic style that no other standard gauge preserved railway in Britain can match. All of its coaches and three of its four passenger locomotives have impeccable Isle of Wight pedigrees." (Handel Kardas, Portrait of the Isle of Wight Railways, 1998)

On 19th May 2005 the railway welcomed the Queen when she came to open the new recently-built Carriage and Wagon Workshop, a £700,000 project part-funded by the lottery. The restoration of each carriage costs between £15,000 and £20,000, just for materials.

There are many ways that we can support the steam railway, as volunteers and as visitors. "The railway is staffed mainly by volunteers working both indoors and out on a variety of tasks." said Graham Gibbons. "All applicants are taken on a tour around the railway, shown the various projects and tasks in hand and then invited back for an actual 'hands on' day to look in more detail at their chosen task".

Voluntary tasks include general administration; research, archives and exhibition making for the museum; station guides, booking clerks, porters and other station staff; maintenance of the stations, their estates and gardens; signal and telegraph operators and permanent way and trackside maintenance workers. There is a whole area of volunteering devoted to the maintenance and restoration of the engines, carriages and wagons. Needed skills include administration, workshop maintenance, painting, upholstery, carpentry. Boilermakers, locomotive fitters, welders and other machine shop trades are in special demand.

If you can offer a little time please contact the Volunteer Co-ordinators at the IW Steam Railway, Havenstreet, PO33 4DS or telephone on 882204. They can advise on transport.

# THE MEN WHO WOULD
# NOT TURN BACK

On the 9th and 10th of March 1888 the volunteer crews of the Brighstone and Brook lifeboats went to the rescue of the 31 people aboard the *Sirenia*. Both the lifeboats were swamped, both the second Coxswains and the Brighstone Coxswain were drowned, and both lifeboat crews knocked out of action. The final deliverance was carried out by a scratch crew drawn from across the Island.

*A rowing lifeboat just after the moment of launching. The technique of launching was particularly difficult, requiring exact timing, according to the length and width and speed of the incoming waves. It required instantaneous co-ordination between the Coxswain, crew, horses and scores of launchers. Courtesy of Dr Robin McInnes OBE.*

"On the morning of the 9th March 1888 there was a dense fog and a surprisingly heavy sea" wrote Major General John Seely, the 1st Lord Mottistone and member of the Brook lifeboat crew. "It often happens on our coast, the Isle of Wight, that when a fog comes down without a breath of wind great rollers come tumbling in; first with a boom like distant thunder as occasional waves break on the outer ledges; then with a loud continuous roar, as the waves from the Atlantic increase in size so that each one breaks on the outer ledge, and then, pressed forward by its follower gathers impetus to hurl itself on the shore. Meanwhile there is still the uncanny absence of wind to account for this great disturbance of the sea." "I was on a job building a barn for my father" Brighstone lifeboatman Robert Buckett later recalled. "The fog was very thick, and the sea made that noise that I suppose it was in the heads of all of us that we hoped the life-boat would not be wanted."

*An oil painting of the Sirenia ashore on Atherfield Ledge by F.J.Edwards.*

Out to sea the three-masted full-rigged ship *Sirenia* of Glasgow wallowed in the ocean swell under full sail. She was close to the end of a long voyage from San Francisco, via Cape Horn, with a cargo of American wheat bound for Dunkirk. She was a big modern ship, displacing 1,588 tons and manned by a crew of 25 under Captian MacIntyre. In addition she carried the captain's wife, their three children and a female servant. Like so many other captains MacIntyre assumed he was sailing south of the Island when in fact the incoming Channel tide had drawn the ship into the twelve mile shallow bay that is formed by the eroded south west coast of the Island. Jutting south into the Channel this coast took an annual harvest of wreck from the busy Channel highway. Typically the cliffs and the lighthouses were buried in fog, and typically the incoming tide guided the *Sirenia* onto the ship killing rocks of the "dreaded Atherfield Ledge", the most dangerous feature of this long perilous coastline; a complex shambles of rock slabs, ridges, boulders and reefs. At about 3pm the *Sirenia* struck hard on the outer ledge, around a mile off the coast.

Atherfield Point was about the most isolated place on the south west coast, and this coast, known as the "Back of the Wight" was the most remote part of the Island, linked only by a handful of lanes that climbed over the Island's steep chalk spine to the villages of Brighstone, Brook, Shorwell and Chale. There was no "Military Road" just crude farm lanes reaching out from the villages to the windswept coastal fields. Some of the locals, known as longshoremen, made part of their living from fishing, salvage and smuggling. For generations they risked their lives to save shipwrecked mariners along this dreadful coast. As the size of ships increased in the Nineteenth Century, so did the need for more sophisticated rescue services. From the 1820s the Coastguard played an increasing role in lifesaving and the new light-houses were built at St Catherines (1840) and the Needles (1859). In 1860 the Royal National Lifeboat Institution had established two stations in the nearest possible spots to Atherfield, at Brook and Brighstone Grange chines.

On the shore that afternoon at Atherfield, young Harry Cotton heard something strange above the roar of the breakers and looked out to sea to what seemed to be a white cloud in the thick fog. Then he realised what it was, a ship ashore still under full sail. There was not a moment to lose. Cotton clambered straight up the muddy seventy-five foot cliff and ran to his father. William "Rufus" Cotton was another member of the Brighstone life-boat crew. He jumped from his chair, grabbed "the usual mouthful of bread and cheese" and set off to raise the alarm. At 4pm the Brighstone lifeboat cannon roared back at the thundering sea.

Already established 28 years, the Brighstone and Brook lifeboat crews were among the most experienced and best equipped in the country. When the Brighstone Station received the new 10 oar *Worcester Cadet* in 1880 its crews had already saved 187 lives. That year Second Coxswain Moses Munt, who had served in the crew for twenty years became the new Coxswain. In 1886 the Coxswain of Brook, John Hayter, was awarded the RNLI Silver Medal after 26 years service in which time his crews had rescued 84 lives. On February 1st, just weeks before the *Sirenia* disaster, the Brook station received the new 10 oar *William Slaney Lewis*. Both stations now had the latest, 30 foot; unsinkable, unbreakable, self-righting lifeboats. However this made them extraordinarily heavy, and very difficult to launch, sail and row.

*The Brighstone Lifeboat Worcester Cadet on her carriage with her volunteer crew and the officers of the local committee. Courtesy of the late Geoff Cotton.*

The mobilisation of the two life-boats used up almost all the available local human resources "... for every able bodied man who can pull an oar is needed, since the numbers in our community are so few." The rest of the available human population was needed for the launch, Seely estimated the ideal number at eighty but this was rare. In addition the lifeboat carriage needed ten farm horses to be manoeuvred into the launch position. They trembled in terror as the freezing cold March seas washed around their legs yet obeyed orders better than in the field. They seemed to understand the importance of the task.

With remarkable speed the Worcester Cadet's carriage was backed into the breakers, Coxswain Munt staring out to sea from the stern, the oarsman facing landwards, their ten massive oars pointing out sideways as if in a salute, the scores of helpers taking the strain on the launch ropes. The waves crashing onshore were now bigger than ever. "I had been out in the boat often before in big storms of wind" recalled Buckett "but I never saw such a big sea breaking on the beach as then."

Coxswain Munt's judgement was critical. Not only had he to choose exactly the right wave, but also the exact moment. The time was 4.15pm. "Launch!" yelled Munt and the helpers ashore heaved on the ropes that shot the lifeboat into and over the oncoming wave. The oars struck the sea in unison, once, twice and then over the crest of the next wave. The *Worcester Cadet* now struggled out to sea. The lack of wind meant that Munt could not use sail. The crew would have to row all the way continually turning to face massive seas. Seely compared the conditions to being under an artillery barrage, as the threat of death confronted the volunteers every half minute. Up the coast, Coxswain John Hayter did not even attempt to launch from Brook Chine.

*The Nineteenth Century saw the rapid development of services to save life from shipwreck. This is how the St Catherine's Lighthouse originally looked. It was later shortened. St Catherine's started operation in 1840. The Needles Lighthouse was completed in 1859. In the 1830s the Island invented the rescue rocket which was issued to the island Coastguards who also carried out boat and cliff rescues. The Coastguard continue to co-ordinate all the local modern sea rescue services.*
*St Catherine's Lighthouse by George Brannon. Courtesy of Dr Robin McInnes OBE.*

The lifeboat carriage was instead dragged down to Grange Chine and reversed into the sea. "Launch!" yelled Hayter, but for all his 28 years experience the *William Slaney Lewis* was picked up like a toy and thrown down against the beach, her crew washed out of her. Two of them were badly injured, several oars were shattered. It would take an hour to restore the lifeboat to her carriage. By this time Munt was closing on the wreck of the Sirenia. The hull of the ship was badly holed and filled with water, the 31 people aboard forced to shelter on the forecastle. The lifeboat attached a line to the fore-rigging and for an hour the lifeboat rose and fell as Mrs MacIntyre, the servant, an apprentice and the three children were lowered by rope into the lifeboat, the smallest, a baby, in a wicker laundry basket. As each incoming sea filled the lifeboat, MacIntyre and Munt had a yelled conversation and agreed that the lifeboat should return at low tide when conditions might have improved.

After a long difficult voyage back to shore Munt beached the *Worcester Cadet* at 6.30pm high on the wave-thrashed Atherfield shore where the Brighstone helpers were waiting. During the voyage of the lifeboat they had pulled the carriage overland and somehow manhandled it over and down the face of the crumbling clay cliffs. Thanks to their magnificent effort the *Worcester Cadet* was again readied for launch. Reunited, the crew and helpers stood drenched, frozen and aching, miles from a change of dry clothes, watching the twenty foot waves explode over the distant *Sirenia's* stern as darkness fell. Meanwhile the Brook boat and carriage had been dragged out of Grange Chine back to the narrow gorge of Chilton Chine where Hayter hoped he could better manage the incoming rollers. Helpers and crew hacked their way through the undergrowth and down the slippery chine manhandling the heavy carriage and lifeboat. Two helpers suffered broken arms.

It was dark now; conditions were getting worse. At 11pm Coxswain Hayter yelled "Launch!" and the *William Slaney Lewis* finally rose on a rushing breaker and pulled out into deep water. But her crew's trials had only just begun. In the mountainous seas now running in the bay it would take several hours hard rowing and sailing to cover the six miles to the wreck, with continuous manoeuvring to meet each incoming wave. After midnight the Brighstone crew at Atherfield noticed the wind was finally coming "First just a gust or two from the south, then a real south-wester" At 1am "Munt guessed right again and we made a fine launch." Now they could raise sail but the wind had increased the power of the huge incoming waves. The lifeboat grappled onto the *Sirenia's* fore rigging with a three inch thick hawser, but this was snapped by a passing wave.

The *Worcester Cadet* struggled back to the ship and attached a thicker line. "The captain hailed us from the rail and told us that we could take off the whole of his crew in two trips. He had thirteen men ready to jump in." Buckett continues, "The sea was very heavy. Sometimes our boat was level with the rail, the next moment she was twenty feet below. In spite of all our efforts to fend her off, we hit her three times with such force that I thought that our boat must be broken to bits. I think we broke at least ten oars in trying to get the boat alongside. But thirteen men managed to jump in, or slide down a rope." "When the last of the thirteen men was on board, Munt shouted out to the bowman to cut us adrift. I turned and repeated the order, and as I turned I saw a great wave in the dim light coming at us. It was worse than any of the others, like a mountain of black water, with a fringe of white on top. Just as the bowman cut the last strand, the wave was on us. I could see it was about to break. Up went the bow, higher and higher, while I held on to the thwart. I could see Munt and the thirteen men tumbling onto him just straight below me..."

The *Worcester Cadet* was carried at this perpendicular angle for a hundred yards, completely out of control. As the wave finally passed under the boat she was struck by a cross sea bouncing off some feature of the ledge. She was swamped from the starboard and capsized. When she righted herself with a jerk 22 of the 26 men managed to clamber back into her. Among the four missing were Moses Munt and the Second Coxswain, Thomas Cotton. Reduced to four oars the survivors "managed to pull back towards the wreck, but could see no sign of Munt or Cotton. We shouted and burnt a flare, but in that great sea it is no wonder we could not see them." The *Worcester Cadet* returned to shore at 2.30am. One of the crew, Frank Downer, was disentangled from the ropes around the bow, along with the corpse of a young American seaman, Leonard Dozier. The body of Moses Munt washed ashore nearby shortly after. It would be another two days before Thomas Cotton's body was found at Blackgang Chine. The Brighstone crew was effectively finished, both officers dead and eight men knocked out with broken bones and exhaustion, including Buckett. As some helpers assisted the survivors from the beach, others began to get the indestructible *Worcester Cadet* ready for another launch.

The *William Slaney Lewis* was now closing on the *Sirenia*, running before the gale, with Second Coxswain Reuben Cooper holding the sweep oar at the stern. John Hayter had steered the lifeboat through "a veritable hell of waters" but just 300 yards from the wreck another massive sea crashed into the lifeboat washing away Ben and Phil Jacobs and Reuben Cooper. Luckily the Jacobs brothers remained attached to life-lines and were hauled, spluttering, aboard.

Cooper's cries for help could be clearly heard from both the lifeboat and the *Sirenia*. Hayter hailed MacIntyre and offered to take off the remaining crew but MacIntyre insisted that they continue the search for Cooper. MacIntyre sent up blue flares to assist Hayter as the Brook men bucked and dived across the chaotic waters of the Atherfield Ledge in the direction of Cooper's last cries. They "were pounded and drenched by huge breakers". Several of the oars were shattered. They failed to find Cooper; his body was never found, and having crossed to the wrong side of the Atherfield Ledge, the exhausted crew were unable to row or sail back.

Defeated, Hayter dropped anchor in Chale Bay to wait for the dawn. Through the remainder of that long night the Brook crew huddled under the sail drenched, frozen, hungry and thirsty; as their little lifeboat ducked and reared, filling with each incoming sea. Dawn came. There was no change in the storm. Hayter raised the anchor and the muscles of the oarsmen burned as they pulled the *William Slaney Lewis* back across the frenzied leaping fury of the Atherfield Ledge, towards the doomed wreck far out on the outer ledge. The people ashore frantically yelled and signalled for them to call off the attempt. Hayter ignored them, but as the lifeboat closed on the *Sirenia* he could see that his crew were simply incapable of further effort, let alone a difficult rescue of thirteen men. He had also seen the *Worcester Cadet* ready for launching. The *William Slaney Lewis* suddenly raised sail and to the relief of those ashore began to beat back to the Brook station. After she beached later that day, it was noted that she had been at sea for fifteen hours.

Back at Atherfield a new lifeboat crew was taking shape. Rufus Cotton, who had raised the alarm the previous day, was elected the new Coxswain. Two other members of the original crew were prepared to make a third attempt. They were David Cotton and the teenager Frank Salter. Some tried to dissuade him. "Let me have a drink of tea and I can manage" he replied. John Cotton of Brighstone, Walter White and Percy Wheeler of Blackgang were about the only local men left to take their places at the oars. Luckily news of the *Sirenia* had spread and longshoremen were arriving from all over the Island. Charles Orchard and the notorious smuggler Fred Bastiani came up from Niton. Charles Kemp, Arthur Sothcott and William Buckett made their way from Sandown and George Spencer from Ventnor. Most remarkable of all, the Coxswain of the Bembridge Lifeboat, George Attrill, had walked fifteen miles into the gale in heavy seaboots to offer his services at the oars.

At noon, at Cotton's command "Launch!" the *Worcester Cadet* lurched forward a third time into the breakers. The scratch crew battled their way out to the tattered wreck and one by one took the twelve remaining crew and Captain MacIntrye on board. After two hours of rising and plummeting on the continuing huge waves the Brighstone boat beached at Atherfield to the hoarse cheers of the onlookers with her precious human cargo intact.

The RNLI held an enquiry into the disaster. John Hayter was exonerated for his handling of the Brook boat and he was awarded a clasp to his silver medal. Moses Munt was also praised for his judgement; he could not have seen the giant wave. All three men who dared go out a third time received the RNLI Silver Medal, £300 was given for the families of the deceased and the proud gravestones of the three corpses found were paid for.

The public response to the disaster was typical. A revolutionary new cliff-face-descent lifeboat station was funded by Island donations and opened at Atherfield on October 29th 1891. Rufus Cotton become Coxswain of the new *Catherine Swift*. Just three months later the *Catherine Swift*, the *Worcester Cadet* and the *William Slaney Lewis* rescued 379 people from the German liner *Eider* in heavy seas on the Atherfield Ledge. The rowing lifeboats of the Back of the Wight continued to provide an important service until 1937.

Over 77 years they were together responsible for saving 826 lives. They were replaced by the motorised lifeboat station at Yarmouth, founded in 1924. Yarmouth is still one of the busiest stations in the country and in recent years has been augmented by the Freshwater Inshore Lifeboat. Both the RNLI and the independent Inshore Lifeboat are manned by volunteers and entirely funded by donations, so when you have the opportunity, remember the men who refused to turn back, and give generously whenever you can.

# FRESHWATER'S FORGOTTEN REMEMBERED

On Friday, November 10th 2006 a private ceremony took place at the Memorial Hall in Freshwater to rededicate the Small Hall to the memory of one of the greatest military tragedies in the Island's modern history. The "Great War" of 1914-18 was the greatest human disaster in the Island's long history. Of all the Island communities remembering the vast scale of sacrifice in the First World War, none suffered more than the parish of Freshwater. In addition to the usual regiments that align the columns of names on the village war memorial in the churchyard; the county regiments, navy and air force; Freshwater lost its entire territorial army unit. The seventy-five names of the Fifth Hampshire Howitzer Battery are recorded separately on the wall of the Main Hall of the Memorial Hall in Avenue Road. Freshwater's 5th Hants Howitzer Battery had the singular misfortune to be incorporated into the only British army to be entirely annihilated in the First World War.

*The British Army finally enter Baghdad in March 1917 after an intense struggle of two and half years that cost the British-Indian Army 92,000 casualties. Courtesy of H.J.Edwards.*

The story of the lost VI Division is seldom told. It is one of those embarrassing military disasters that we as a nation prefer to forget. It was a tale in which generals and government were completely tarnished. It is also a story of unimaginable horror. The only saving grace is that we know from survivors that the victims remained loyal to one another and somehow maintained their personal morality and dignity. The young men of Freshwater who volunteered for the Territorial Army prior to the war were trained as artillery men with a mobile unit of howitzers, guns aiming into the sky to drop shells vertically on the enemy. They trained at Freshwater Drill Hall which had been built by public subscription. The foundation stone had been dedicated by Hallam, 2nd Lord Tennyson, in 1899. In August 1914 the Territorial Army was mobilized, generally for home defence, or to go with the professional army to fight the German armies invading Belgium and France. However, by some vagary of the War Office the 5th Battery was assigned to the VI (Poona) Division of the British Indian Army.

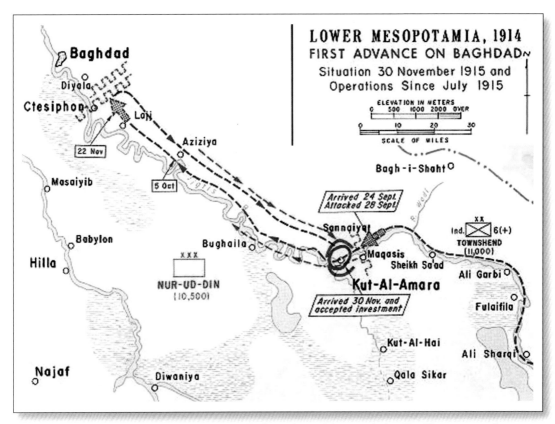

*The campaign from the capture of Kut to the Battle of Ctesiphon and the retreat back to Kut. The map was made at The United States Military Academy at West Point.*

## The Invasion of Iraq

This division was to be the striking force for the British invasion of Iraq, then three provinces of the Turkish Ottoman Empire. In October 1914 The Ottoman Empire joined the war on the German side. As Iraq had begun to produce oil which was essential for the Royal Navy, the British Army in India immediately invaded, taking Basra on November 22nd 1914. After securing the Persian Gulf the VI Division began to fight its way upstream along the Tigris and Euphrates, into a roadless expanse of marshes, desert and mud towards Baghdad.

Although outclassed by superior British military technology the Turkish infantry fought stubbornly in an endless series of defensive battles. According to the book *"Remembering Kut"* by Davina Neave, a copy of which is dedicated to the men of the Memorial Hall, "Conditions were worse than those experienced on any other front... tropical heat and diseases, flood flies and mud". Every year the inland marshes flooded into an inland sea. Sometimes the Division attacked in a flotilla of 500 river boats, sometimes on dry land, and sometimes waist-deep in clinging mud, beset by clouds of flies by day, mosquitoes by night and plagued by sub-tropical parasites and pests.

Wounds and illness sent thousands of casualties downriver as the logistics supply of food, ammunition and medicine managed from New Delhi became increasingly inadequate. As a result the 15,000 men of the Division began to suffer shortages. The war had brought destitution to an already poor native Arab population who were naturally hostile to the British and Indian invaders. In a country that was beginning to starve, both the Turks and the VI Division were absolutely dependent on their tenuous supply lines.

## The Battle of Ctesiphon

Looking back it would have been wise to rest the offensive but the logic of total war had its own momentum. General Townshend carried on attacking. The troops of the Division advanced for a full twelve months, driving back the Turks from one position to the next until the British were just eighteen miles short of Baghdad. In November 1915 the Turks were reinforced and the British made the mistake of attacking once too often. 14,000 troops attacked 22,000. The two sides fought bitterly for two full days (22-24th November) until the British collapsed back, decisively beaten with a third of their number, 4,500 men, killed or wounded. Neave called the battle of Ctesiphon "one of the greatest blunders of this deplorable campaign".

Riverboats groaning with wounded steamed downstream as the formations of the Division marched along the banks in headlong retreat. The Division fell back a full hundred miles, sweeping up reinforcements and garrison detachments. By the time the infantry and artillery were finally surrounded in the town of Kut by the Turks (the cavalry had escaped) the army had 15,759 men, 3,152 British and 12,607 Indians. In the town with them were about 6,000 Arab civilians. On December 3rd 1915 one of the greatest sieges of the First World War began.

## The Siege of Kut

Kut was closely besieged with trenchworks and battered with artillery. The Turks made repeated attacks. This was bitter trench warfare, trenches sometimes fully flooded, without quarter to bury the dead. They were left to fester in the beating sun, their stench adding misery to the slow starvation of both armies. General Townshend assumed that the IV Division would quickly be relieved as other divisions advanced from the coast. However the Turks had pushed far down river to Amara, and once dug-in inflicted defeat after defeat on the British army.

Four times the British-Indian army advanced to relieve the VI Division and four times it was defeated, with total casualties of 26,000 men, double the number incarcerated at Kut. The epic siege lasted for five months. By the time the VI Division requested terms of surrender the rations consisted of "the sweeping of bins, full of husks and muddy dirt". General Townshend tried to bribe the Turkish premier with a million pound bribe. Enver Pasha refused.

The Turks offered generous terms by which all the remaining troops could be evacuated in return for their surviving cannon. General Townshend refused. Instead the British destroyed all their remaining artillery. These included the last howitzer of the Freshwater Battery. In 1930 a piece of the gun's tail was found and returned to the Memorial Hall where it serves as a grisly reminder of the lost battery. The Turks allowed a thousand British-Indian wounded to be taken downriver on ships leaving 12,300 men to march out of the town on April 29th as prisoners of war. If they had known then what would happen to them many would probably have preferred to cut their own throats. What they had just survived was nothing to the suffering they were about to endure.

## The Death March

According to the rules of war the officers, including the medical doctors, were treated separately, and sent to a fairly privileged captivity. General Townshend was accommodated in a palace on an island off Istanbul. The rank and file were at a stroke deprived of the officer corps who had always taken care of them. The rank and file were now to follow the orders of the Turkish army, but this army was hardly able to feed itself as the cycle of war, economic collapse, starvation and anarchy spun uncontrollably out of control. One British soldier noted that their captors, the Turkish soldiers "were literally starving... their own sick and wounded were treated no better than our own."

The pattern of life as prisoners soon dawned on the captive soldiers. They could barely be fed or sheltered, there was nothing to be had. Rather they would be robbed of their superior boots and clothes by their captors, beaten and humiliated and sent on a march of death towards the heart of an empire that was going into a moral and political meltdown. By the time the forced march to Baghdad was completed over one sixth of the captives, 2,200 men, had died, their corpses lining the road. Another 1,250 died at the US Consulate where the Consul offered them the last outside care they would ever receive before the Consul himself died from the cholera caught from the sick soldiers. The march continued, through northern Iraq towards the Taurus Mountains. The British and Indian survivors suffered dreadfully, as Neave describes it "in the terrible midsummer heat, provided with next to no food and with great scarcity of water with no transport for those that fell sick... dragged and flogged on the march, clubbed and left to die on the roadside in a country infested by brigands." By the time his column reached Mosul one Private Metcalfe recalls "Not one of the prisoners had a boot left and next to no clothes."

## Death in the Labour Camps

By now we have statistically lost sight of the VI Division which was now split up into work parties. From the British government point of view these troops were a disgrace as they had surrendered and almost no effort was made to exchange prisoners or to find out what happened to them. Just 209 men were exchanged. The newspapers suppressed this inglorious story. The Red Cross could not access the remaining prisoners. For the Turkish government, invaded on all sides and engaged in the genocide of over a million of its Armenian citizens, the fate of a few thousand prisoners was irrelevant. It is assumed that more than half the men who marched out of Kut in April 1915 were dead by late October. For the next two years the survivors worked in labour camps, still on starvation rations, on railways, roads and docks. One corporal records his party being kept labouring on a road "from 6am to 6pm many dying on their feet". "We lost according to reports" recalls another survivor at another labour camp "eighty odd men in the first month and one hundred and eighty odd in the second".

## Aftermath

In late 1918 the Ottoman Empire disintegrated and the war came to an end. Some survivors did make it back to Freshwater. I heard one tale of a girl who followed a man from Freshwater Railway Station in the early 1920s. To her surprise he walked to her home. He turned out to be her brother, a man she no longer recognised. The Commonwealth War Graves Commission collected as many of the bodies as they could and buried them in a cemetery near Baghdad. The seventy five names of the 5th Battery are recorded on plaques in the Freshwater Memorial Hall and Newport Drill Hall.

# TUDOR FORTS

*Cowes Castle was built in 1539. In 1642 the first shot of the English Civil War was fired by the fort's royalist commander against HMS Lion which like the rest of the navy, sided with Parliament. The navy quickly responded by seizing all the Island's castles from their royalist officers. In 1858 the decommissioned castle became the permanent home of the Royal Yacht Squadron.*
*Courtesy of Dr Robin McInnes OBE.*

*Yarmouth Castle as it appeared in the eighteenth Century.*
*The castle was completed and operational in 1547 two years after the Battle of Portsmouth.*
*Courtesy of Isle of Wight Records Office.*

# ISLAND BEFALLEN

*The Royal Marine Hotel was among a number of significant Island buildings destroyed by German aerial bombing in the Second World War. Courtesy of Dr Robin McInnes OBE.*

*The spectacular old Undercliff Road from Niton to Blackgang was lost following the great landslide of 1928. Courtesy of Dr Robin McInnes OBE.*

# THE BATTLE OF COWES

On the night of the 4/5th May sixty-five years ago the stillness of the night over the blacked-out town of Cowes was shattered by the most merciless onslaught on the Island in 400 years. Through the night hundreds of German bombers directed a hail of bombs onto the burning town. Thankfully one warship stood at the centre of the spirited defence, and saved the town along with the sheer courage of the rest of the defence forces. During the Second World War (1939-45) the Island was on the front line from the Fall of France in June 1940 to the Normandy Landings of July 1944. The Island was a frequent target of aerial bombing attacks, and particularly Cowes, the Island's most important industrial town, producing warships and military aircraft at the greatest speed possible. After the daytime Battle of Britain in 1940 the German Luftwaffe and British Royal Air Force adopted the tactic of intensive night bombing of towns and cities. Air raid alerts were a frequent occurrence in Cowes.

*The Cowes built Polish destroyer Blyskawica is now preserved as a museum piece in the port of Gdynia.*

On March 28th 1942 234 RAF bombers attacked the wooden built medieval city of Lubeck with incendiaries. The annihilation of the pretty town infuriated the German High Command and intensive raids were ordered on secondary British targets, including Cowes. The devastation in Cowes could have been significantly worse was it not for the fortuitous presence of the Polish Destroyer, ORP *Blyskawica* ("Lightning", pronounced 'bliskaviska'). This particularly heavily armed 372 foot destroyer had been built in the J. Samuel White's shipyard and launched in 1936. In 1939 she escaped from the German invasion of Poland to serve in the Royal Navy. In early 1942 she was sent to her home port to have new bofors guns fitted.

The *Blyskawica* docked at J. Samuel White's on April 11th near to the chain ferry as yet another air raid siren began to wail. She came under repeated aerial attacks. Her captain Commander Wojciech Roman Francki asked the Admiralty if he could keep the ship armed while in dock. The Admiralty refused. As Francki later recalled, "Taking matters into my own hands I ordered more ammunition aboard".

The ship with her guns at the ready, manned by her battle-hardened crew, proved to be a decisive factor in the ensuing battle. Early in the night of May 4th the townsfolk of Cowes would hear the familiar warning siren that so often foretold the sight and rumbling sound of passing aircraft en route to inland targets. However, unbeknown to them it would be their turn to be the focal point of the attack.

## Cowes Under Attack

Michael Zawada had been ordered to join the crew of No. 6 Bofors gun on the *Blyskawica*. At approximately 10.40pm he noticed searchlights and the sound of aircraft approaching. The first waves of 160 low flying fighter-bombers began the onslaught on Cowes. Although the town was blacked out it was easy to make out the target because of the shape of the coast and the Medina estuary. The first warplanes dropped a string of parachute flares from west to east over the Saunders Roe factory. Others followed dropping a mixture of high explosives and incendiaries and strafing with their machine-guns. "Fires started everywhere and in a few minutes Cowes became an inferno and the fire brigade had a horrible job in front of them" recalled Zawada.

"The sky which had been clear began to cloud over as the fires started to burn and more bombs fell… it was bright as daylight although it was night". Zawada was impressed by "the sheer courage and guts these firemen exhibited in pulling people from burning buildings and putting out fires while bombs rained down upon them" From its position at the shipyard the *Blyskawica* was the mainstay in the town's defence, providing a central focus for the local anti-aircraft artillery, incessantly using its heavy calibre guns to keep the Luftwaffe aircraft high and in doing so denying them greater accuracy with their bombs.

"The bombers could not withstand the intensity of our fire" recalls Commander Francki, "and were forced to divert to either side". Further south, Free French naval units stationed on the Medina opened fire with smaller calibre weapons, illustrating the truly multinational nature of the defence. For two hours the German bombs rocked the town with heart stopping explosions. The night filled with the scream of falling bombs and diving aircraft, the smell of explosives mixed with vaporised brickdust, the thud of anti-aircraft guns firing, the rattle of machine-gun fire. In the communal bomb shelters people muttered prayers and sang hymns. The gun barrels of the anti-aircraft guns glowed red in the night as they blasted into the sky. The crew of the *Blyskawica* threw raised buckets of water from the river to cool them.

Yet it was clear that the defence was working, the bombs were falling to the south of the main target, south of the blazing destroyer and the pall of smoke over the dockyards. Many of the incendiaries had fallen into Parkhurst Forest confusing the later waves of bombers with great fires far to the south of the town and some thousands of incendiaries fell harmlessly into the marshes of the estuary where they failed to explode. The attack was nonetheless a devastating one, and by the time the bombers returned to their bases to refuel and rearm, the town was stricken.

As the battle abated attention turned to the emergency services which had been in action since the start of the bombing, fighting the fires, searching for people buried in the rubble, identifying unexploded bombs, passing messages. The Womens Voluntary Service (WVS) opened eight centres for the homeless while the wounded were carried to Northwood House. In East Cowes the wounded were taken to the Frank James Hospital. By the end of the night the corridors were full of stretchers and new casualties were taken to Osborne House Convalescent Home.

*The result of the bombing in Cowes. Courtesy of the East Cowes Heritage Centre.*

## The Second Wave

Feelings of relief at having survived the initial attack were quickly dissipated as the sound of the returning bombers could be heard at around 2am. The German aircraft repeated the attack with flares, high explosive and incendiary bombs, laying siege to the town for another frightful two hour stretch. Missiles rained down on the town, with one huge bomb creating an enormous crater which held the remains of two air raid shelters at the corner of Yarborough and King's Roads in East Cowes. "Suddenly we were aware of yet another screaming bomb" recalls Maisie Frampton, then ten years old "but this one was different – the noise was deafening as it appeared to get closer and then for a second 'dead silence'… My father leaned across and took my hand and my mother leaned across me." Of the 23 people cowering in that shelter "only three survived, my mother, my cousin and I".

Nearby Mrs Hann a butcher's wife serving with the WVS refused to abandon her post providing refreshments for the firemen at Minerva Boat Yard. Her van was found blown to pieces. With her died two Ryde firemen. The defences on that harrowing night did the town proud. A number of the attacking aircraft were shot down. Nettlestone and Whippingham anti aircraft batteries are both credited with shooting down two bombers. Later RAF night fighters shot down four of the warplanes as they returned to their airfields.

## The Aftermath

When daybreak arrived on the 5th May, a beautiful spring day, help continued to pour into Cowes from emergency volunteer services from all over the Island. The crew of the *Blyskawica* now turned into teams of firemen and diggers supporting the tireless efforts of the local emergency teams. The wounded were carried away to Newport and Ryde.

IN MEMORY OF THOSE WHO LOST THEIR LIVES
IN AIR RAIDS ON THIS TOWN 1939-1945.

INTERRED IN THIS GRAVE ARE

| | | |
|---|---|---|
| WILLIAM ADAMS | SALLIE COSTER | EMILY MARY LAIDLER |
| JESSIE M ADAMS | MARION COSTER | EDWARD HENRY MAKER |
| WILLIAM BROADWATER | PETER VIVIAN COSTER | DORA MABEL MAKER |
| NAOMI BROADWATER | GEORGE F. DEACON | ANNIE TROTTER MOORE |
| ERNEST C BURGESS | LILIAN LUCY DEACON | CHARLES A PRITCHARD |
| MABEL LUCY BURGESS | JEAN MARGARET DEACON | MARIA ANNE PRITCHARD |
| HILDA LILIAN COLSON | ROBERT FRANK GALTON | FRED SAMUEL POLLEY |
| HERBERT COOK | FLORENCE E. GALTON | EMMA ROWE |
| MARY COOK | MAUREEN J. GALTON | SAMUEL RUSSELL |
| JAMES HENRY COOKE | HERBERT LOUIS HODGE | MADELINE AMY RUSSELL |
| EILEEN DORIS COOKE | MARJORIE W. JEANS | ANNIE MAUD SUMNER |
| VALERIE ANN COOKE | ANNE ELIZABETH JEANS | FLORENCE M.SUMNER |
| JEANETTE E. COOKE | EDWARD ARTHUR KERSEY | GEORGE HENRY SYKES |
| VIVIENNE C.COOKE | RUBY MAY KERSEY | EMILY MARY WHEELER |
| | RAYMOND ARTHUR KERSEY | |

ELSEWHERE IN THIS CEMETERY ARE

| | | |
|---|---|---|
| GLADYS MAISIE CLARK | FRANK WILLIAM HARVEY | TERENCE NEIL PAINE |
| CHARLES A.HALLIDAY | RONALD MILLMORE | ALBERT WINSOR |
| JOHN M HALLIDAY | MABEL J. MILLMORE | |

INTERRED IN OTHER PLACES ARE

| | | |
|---|---|---|
| FREDERICK BARTLETT | DENNIS M.BARTLETT | WILLIAM ERNEST GLASS |
| IRIS MAY BARTLETT | | ALICE FRANCES HANN |

*This memorial in the cemetery at East Cowes displays all those East Cowes residents who lost their lives during World War II.*
*The wreaths shown are to commemorate the 65th anniversary of the Battle of Cowes 5th May 1942.*
*Courtesy of Friends of East Cowes Cemetery.*

For the dazed people of the port towns the full extent of the devastation was now revealed. 200 tons of explosives had been dropped on the two towns. The East Cowes ship yards along the river and the SARO aircraft works in West Cowes were completely demolished. Some streets were covered with steep heaps of rubble. In both towns of Cowes streets were sealed off to deal with delayed time tombs. Many homes had been destroyed or were uninhabitable. It is said that a thousand people were made homeless in a single street. All worked tirelessly searching for bodies, unexploded bombs, cleaning up and taking care of the mass of refugees and workers. It is estimated that the WVS provided 25,000 meals in the next few days.

In total – and in spite of the countless efforts of bravery from defence workers – more than 70 people lost their lives in the attacks. Nevertheless much of the two towns of Cowes had been saved. Memorials to the dead were built in both towns.

When the *Blyskawica* was finally decommissioned in 1976, she was preserved as a museum ship in Gdynia in Poland. In 2002, the courage of the ship's crew was formally recognised and commemorated by the people of Cowes, marking the 60th anniversary of the attacks. At another ceremony on May 3rd, 2004, Commander Francki's daughter, Nina Doroszkowska, unveiled a special plaque which named the area outside the Painter's Arms "Francki Place" and commemorated both the foresight of the Captain and the bravery of his crew.

Today, vivid memories of the attack are fading, with fewer and fewer people who experienced the attacks still living in Cowes. However, the terror of the 4/5th May and the astounding bravery of the defence workers should never be forgotten.

# THE ROCKET MEN OF THE NEEDLES

As a child I remember my face and hands pressed against the metal fence looking through at the forbidden Needles Headland. The Island's space programme was open knowledge but there was a certain hush on this top-secret project. In the 1950s and '60s hundreds of scientists and engineers successfully built, assembled and tested "perhaps the most economical and powerful space missile of its time - the Black Knight." Their work climaxed in 1971 with the launch of the first, and last, all-British satellite launched by a British rocket, Black Arrow. It was a huge technical success. The atomic missiles and space rockets were developed in a few years of intense intellectual engineering expertise. It was also vastly expensive for a bankrupt, shrinking British Empire and abruptly terminated at the moment of crowning success.

*A test firing of Black Knight at the Needles test site.*
*This illustration does not take into account that the British rockets had no flame wake and made little sound.*
*The "fountain of steam" was made of vaporised water used to cool the rocket in the test firing.*
*Courtesy of the National Trust.*

Had we persisted with the *Black Knight*, instead of buying the US *Polaris* system, perhaps Britain would now be as free in foreign policy as the French, with their independent bomb, rather than being tied to US foreign policy. If we had followed up on *Black Arrow* we certainly could have remained at the centre of the European space industry, launching hundreds of commercial satellites into space, rather than paying for loads on the French *Ariane*.

*This photograph of a launch of a Black Arrow at the Woomera Space Station in Australia shows the smokeless take off using the novel hydrogen peroxide and kerosene fuel. Courtesy of The National Trust.*

In the 1950s Britain was still a "great power" with a large empire and quickly followed the new "superpowers" the USA and USSR in developing the atomic and hydrogen bomb, testing them in Australia. These weapons now needed a delivery system. The British government ordered the invention and construction of an inter-continental ballistic missile, code named "*Blue Streak*" The job fell to the Royal Aircraft Establishment at Farnborough.

They began an intense effort to research, marshal and consolidate the required technology. Their findings particularly drew their attention to engine-makers Armstrong Siddley and Cowes aircraft designers Saunders Roe. The Blue Streak would be preceded by a smaller prototype rocket that used the same complex liquid propellants but employed hardware and techniques that were immediately available. This rocket was code named *Black Knight.*

In 1955 Saunders Roe of Cowes were commissioned to develop the air-frame and to carry out the assembly and testing of the missile. Saunders Roe had started life in Cowes in 1901, building light weight high speed boats, moving into seaplane design and production in 1914, culminating in the construction of the beautiful *Princess* flying boats. By 1955 they were developing a mixed power-plant fighter aircraft, the Sr53. This employed a rocket motor which ran on kerosene and high test peroxide. With engine makers Armstrong Siddley, Saunders Roe adapted this motor for space operations and evolved special methods to fabricate the large, lightweight tanks needed to hold the propellant which made up some 90% of the rocket's total mass.

Of special concern was the need to maintain cleanliness and chemical purity when dealing with high-test peroxide which reacts rapidly with most substances by violently separating into very high temperature steam and oxygen. The high test hydrogen peroxide ($H_3O_2$) ignited instantly on contact with kerosene into super heated steam that could propel the missile faster than the speed of sound, but with little sound and an almost invisible flame wake.

## *The Needles Test Site*

To assemble and test each rocket before shipment to the Australian launch site at Woomera, Saunders Roe required a local test site. The former artillery battery on the Needles Headland offered a secure location with underground accommodation. In 1955 the site was leased from the Ministry of War. Here, from April 1956, the engines were assembled, tethered and fired, with different levels of fuel to measure the thrust, flight control systems and the consumption of the fuel.

The Needles Headland was transformed into something like a James Bond film set. A complex of specialised buildings was constructed over the New Battery, and underground control and instrumentation rooms were converted from the old magazines. There were 2,200 square feet of control rooms and underground stores, 4,260 square feet of laboratories and offices and 3,080 square feet of workshops and smaller machine shops. The dining rooms catered for 80 people at a time.

The 60 foot long rockets were assembled in the workshops. Then they were towed down the newly built road along the cliff top above Scratchells Bay to one of the two 80 foot high test gantries. These stood at each side of the natural bowl in the cliff formation above Sun Corner. The rockets were erected inside the steel and aluminium towers by men dressed in protective suits with glass fronted helmets, operating one and a half ton mobile hoists. During an engine firing test all activities followed at a strict time sequence, initially co-ordinated by large clocks placed at all manned positions. At any point the process could be aborted by the press of a button from several monitoring positions.

As the black hands ticked towards the red section of the clock face, the clocks bleeped every ten seconds to warn the workers to get underground. There the scientists stared into an array of "huge grey instrument panels, covered with flickering lights, cathode ray tubes and multi-coloured switches and plugs." In addition to manual observations, an array of cameras, tape recorders and specialised devices automatically logged data from several hundred instrumentation sensors placed within the engine and other rocket systems to assess their performance. On ignition the four jet rocket motors fired into steel "exhaust buckets," cooled by a torrent of water from a specially built 60,000 gallon reservoir, at a rate of 3,000 gallons per minute. The water emerged at right angles from the cliff as "a fountain of steam" as the late Vera Attewell recalled, seeing it from the sea, but it only sounded "like a wet squib."

At this point the only thing stopping the missile flying through the roof of the gantry was a steel golf-ball coupling in the engine structure clamped to the test bed. The local population were warned of the firings and the downs were closed to the public, "as far back as Tennyson's Monument at least once to my knowledge" recalls Derek Mack, who worked on the project throughout. With the missile successfully tested a team of engineers accompanied it to the top security missile launch-site at Woomera in Australia.

In 1958, after just three years work, they released the first *Black Knight* into the atmosphere. In all 22 were launched into moonless night skies, up to 500 miles above the Earth, falling back to land 80-100 miles down-range of the launch site. Despite this success Britain eventually gave up on *Blue Streak* and acquired *Polaris* missiles from the USA. *Black Knight* became a tool for research into the upper atmosphere, flying payloads for government agencies and universities. This work suggested the need for Britain to develop a capacity to launch satellites, which led to the next stage of the space programme.

## The Space Satellite Programme

In 1965 the Needles team started work on *Black Arrow*, an 18 ton, almost 44 foot, three-stage space-rocket designed to put a 300 kilogram satellite into a circular 300 mile orbit. The first two stages were designed to reach the right orbital height; the third blasted the satellite at right angles to the Earth's surface, with sufficient velocity to put it into an orbit of continuous free-fall. Six Black Arrows were built and four launched into space, the first in 1968. The project culminated in October 1971 with the launch of the first, and only, all-British satellite put into space by a British rocket. The experimental satellite *Prospero* achieved a near perfect orbit and carried out short term data collection on micro-meteorites and space erosion.

Having achieved its peak the British space programme suddenly ended in a lack of political will and scientific consensus on how to use the rocket. The Needles rocket site was closed and the buildings dismantled. In 1979 the Woomera station was demilitarised. The concrete bones of the Needles rocket site are one of the few reminders of the successful, but short-lived, British space programme. The headland is now run by the National Trust who cleared the surface of the site down to the concrete foundations when they took it over in the late 1970s.

In recent years the National Trust began to excavate the underground rooms. They have now been re-opened with an exhibition of the Needles Rocket Programme.

Since 1998 a British Rocketing Oral History Programme holds annual conferences to save the memories of the surviving "rocket men" (www.brohp.org.uk). The last Black Arrow now resides at the British Science Museum. Another reminder is *Prospero*, which can still be heard ticking away using the appropriate 1970s equipment. *Prospero* will continue to orbit us for another 220 years.

# CONCLUSION

In my research I have discovered that Island history is a rich field for potential research. As an Island we seem to have accumulated an abundance of historic landscapes and archaeology that is often obliterated elsewhere.

The Island boasts a fossil record from the time of the dinosaurs to mammals and modern man. We have two of the best excavated Roman villas in the country, representing 10% of all Roman villas open to the public in the UK.

We have an intact medieval castle, working water and wind mills, Britain's second oldest light-house and three medieval town centres, one preserved for posterity, frozen in the Fourteenth Century, the others still centres of working towns. Tudor castles, gentry manors, a royal palace, and a large number of town and country dwellings dating from the Seventeenth to Nineteenth centuries are among our outstanding collection of historic architecture.

In addition to the buildings we have our historic landscape, a road network that is thousands of years old, ancient field boundaries and woodland. The archaeological work on the drowned Solent landscape is one of international significance.

We have a great backlog of written records waiting to be researched but sadly we do not have the archaeological and academic staff to research and publish. This is left to individuals with the time, personal resources and the interest to pursue their interests.

There is certainly an interest out there and the Island has the potential to develop a new kind of educational tourism with all types of schools and universities and all ages of interested adults. University archaeological departments should be encouraged to survey the landscape and practice rescue digs. Schools could combine studies of history with geology and geography using the wealth of resources in the landscape and already created by the infrastructure of tourism.

There are thirty museums on the Island catering to the tourist market curious about the Island's history. There is clearly a significant and growing market of visitors to the Island interested in our heritage and history. This influx can support the Island's tourist industry in the quieter months alongside the summer season of cultural events and family holidays. For international tourists the Island could be a way to discover English history in a few days.

There are at least twenty-eight historical associations known to the IW Council. These are popular with both Islanders and with Overners who are keen to understand the heritage, traditions and history of their adopted home. All these resources need encouragement and investment by the Isle of Wight Council. Only with an effective strategy can we achieve the full potential new jobs, products and services that can be of long term benefit to the Island's tourist industry.

Over the next few pages, I have listed some of the resources available where you can find more detailed information about the history of our Island. I hope this book is just a beginning in a process of historical rediscovery.

# For those of you who are interested to find out more here is a list of suggestions.

## Isle of Wight Heritage Service
The Isle of Wight Heritage Service is a department of the Isle of Wight Council. It consists of the County Record Office, the Local Studies Collection, the Museums Service and the Archaeology and Historic Environment Service.

The County Record Office holds collections of primary source documents including deeds, estate records, church registers, maps and illustrations. There are also some local newspapers on microfilm and a card index of entries in surviving parish registers. The Office is open Monday to Friday and an appointment is not always necessary. The County Archivist is Richard Smout

## IW County Record Office
26 Hillside, Newport, IW, PO30 2EB
Tel: 823821 e-mail: record.office@iow.gov.uk
web: www.iwight.com/library/record_office

The Local Studies Collection contains printed material about the Isle of Wight, mainly in book form but with some magazines and pamphlets. The main part of the Collection is housed at Library Headquarters at Somerton near Cowes but some items, such as trade and street directories and electoral registers, are kept at the Record Office (see above). The Collection is available Monday to Friday and although an appointment is not necessary, it is advisable to phone first to see if the Librarian is there. The Librarian is Sheila Caws.

## Library HQ
5 Mariners Way, Somerton, Cowes, IW, PO30 8PD
Tel: 203887 e-mail: local.studies@iow.gov.uk
web: www.iwight.com/thelibrary
(All Island libraries have an Isle of Wight section with collections of varying size and content.)

The Museum Service is responsible for the Museums operated by the Council. These include the Museum of Human History at the Guildhall in Newport, Cowes Maritime Museum, Dinosaur Isle and Newport Roman Villa. Please check for individual opening times. The Curator is Corina Westwood.

## Museum Service
Guildhall, High Street, Newport, IW, PO30 1TY
Tel: 823847 e-mail: museums@iow.gov.uk
web: www.iwight.com/council/departments/museums

The Isle of Wight Archaeology and Historic Environment Service is based in Carisbrooke. Amongst their many responsibilities are the maintenance of the Sites and Monuments Record, a database of important sites on the Island, and the administration of the Portable Antiquities Scheme, a nationwide voluntary scheme for the recording of archaeological objects found by members of the public. The Young Archaeologists Club is one of their most popular activities. Open Monday to Friday but please phone before visiting.

## The County Archaeologist is Ruth Waller.
61 Clatterford Road, Carisbrooke, IW, PO30 1NZ.
Tel: 823810 e-mail: archaeology@iow.gov.uk
web: www.iwight.com/living_here/planning/archaeology

# ISLAND MUSEUMS

The following list of museums is not complete but an indication of the range of different types of museums to be found on the Island.

**Blackgang Chine Heritage Exhibitions.**
Blackgang Chine Pleasure Park. PO38 2HN
Tel: 730330. e-mail: info@blackgang chine.com
Web: www.blackgangchine.com

**Brading Dolls Museum,**
High St. Brading PO36 0DJ.
Tel: 407231

**Brading Experience/Waxworks,**
46-48 High Street, Brading, IW, PO36 0DQ
Tel: 407286
e-mail: info@bradingtheexperience.co.uk

**Brading Roman Villa,**
Morton Old Road, Brading, PO36 OEN.
Tel: 406223.
e-mail: anthony@bradingromanvilla.org.uk
Website : www.bradingromanvilla.org.uk

**Brading Town Museum,**
Old Town Hall, Main Rd. Brading.

**Carisbrooke Castle Museum,**
Carisbrooke Castle, Carisbrooke, Newport, IW PO30 1XY
Tel: 523112. e-mail carismus@lineone.net
Web: www.carisbrookecastlemuseum.org.uk"

**Classic Boat Museum,**
Seaclose Wharf, Town Quay Newport Harbour, PO30 2EF.
Tel: 533493
e-mail: kimlyall@msn.com

**Cowes Maritime Museum,**
Beckford Rd. Cowes. PO31 7SG
Tel: 293394.

**Dimbola Lodge Photographic Museum,**
Terrace Lane, Freshwater Bay, IW, PO40 9QE.
Tel: 756814. E-mail administrator@dimbola.co.uk

**Dinosaur Isle Museum**
Culver Parade, Sandown PO36 8QA
Tel: 404344

**East Cowes Heritage Centre**
Clarence Rd. Open to 1pm
Tel: 280310

**Guildhall Museum of Human History,**
High Street, Newport, IW PO30 1TY.
Tel: 823366

**IW Bus & Coach Museum,**
Seaclose Quay, Newport Harbour, PO30 2EF
Tel: 533352
E-mail: info@iowbusmuseum.org.uk

**IW Geological Museum,**
High Street, Sandown, IW, PO36 8AF
Tel: 404344

**Isle of Wight Military History Museum,**
Northwood Camp, 490 Newport Road, Cowes, IW, PO31 8QU
Tel: 527411

**Longshoremens Museum,**
Esplanade, Ventnor, IW PO38 1JT
Tel: 853176

**National Wireless Museum,**
Arreton Manor, Arreton, PO30 3AA

**Newport Roman Villa,**
Cypress Rd. Newport. PO301HE
Tel: 529720

**Nostalgia Toy Museum,**
High St. Godshill. PO38 3HZ
Tel: 840181

**Shanklin Chine Heritage Centre**
Tel: 866432

**Shell Museum/Natural History Centre,**
High St. Godshill. PO38 3HZ
www.shellmuseum.co.uk

**Sir Max Aitken Museum,**
The Prospect, 83 High Street, Cowes, IW, PO31 7AJ
Tel: 295144

**Ventnor Heritage Museum,**
11 Spring Hill, Ventnor, IW, PO38 1PE
Tel: 855407

For Internet based research the best resource is to be found by searching for
Isle of Wight History Centre

# Historic Buildings

There are also a number of historic buildings on the Island which are sometimes open to the public. Some are in current use and some require contacting beforehand.

**English Heritage Sites**
Appuldurcombe House
Carisbrooke Castle
Osborne House
St Catherines Oratory
Yarmouth Castle

**National Trust Sites**
Bembridge Windmill
Needles Batteries
Newtown Town Hall
Mottistone Manor

**Other places of Historical Interest**
Arreton Manor
Brading Town Hall
Cowes Castle – Royal Yacht Squadron
Morton Manor
Needles Lighthouse
Northwood House
Nunwell House
Ryde Town Hall/Theatre
Sandown Castle (IW Zoo)
St Catherines Lighthouse

# Isle of Wight History Societies

Below is a list of some of the Island's many history societies. For the full addresses and other contact details please visit the online Isle of Wight History Centre by entering it into the Search function or via http://freespace.virgin.net/roger.hewitt/iwias/home.htm.

Details are also available by e-mail from record.office@iow.gov.uk or local.studies@iow.gov.uk or telephone the County Record Office on 823821.

Bembridge Heritage Society:
Brading Town Trust
Brighstone Local History Group
Buildings Preservation Trust
Cowes Group, Isle of Wight Society
Cowes Heritage
East Cowes Heritage
East Cowes Isle of Wight Society
Farringford Tennyson Society:
Friends of Brading Roman Villa
Friends of Carisbrooke Castle Museum
Friends of Royal Osborne:
Historical Association – IW Branch
Historical Vehicle Club
IW Catholic History Society:
IW Church History Society:
IW Family History Society:
IW Gardens Trust:
IW Industrial Archaeology Society:
IW Natural History & Archaeological Society:
IW Postcard Collectors Club
IW Rifles Living History Club
IW Steam Railway Society

IW Young Archaeologists Club
Newchurch Parish History Society:
Newport Group, Isle of Wight Society
Royal Yacht Squadron:
Ryde Social Heritage Group:
St Helens Historical Society
Sandown & District Historical Association:
Shanklin & District Historical Association:
Shorwell Countryside and Heritage Group:
Vectis Searchers:
Ventnor & District Local History Society
Wootton Parish Archive
Wireless Museum
Wolfgard Dark Ages Society
World Ship Society IW Branch
Workers Educational Association:
Yarmouth Society

# Isle of Wight Local History Organisations

**Courtesy of the Isle of Wight History Centre website.**
Please note not all these details are up to date.

**St Helens Historical Society**
Mr J Bacon
The Castle
Duver Road
St Helens
tel: 01983 872164

**Bembridge Heritage Society**
Miss J Plane
42 Howgate Road
Bembridge, PO35 5QW
tel: 10983 872102

**Brading Town Trust**
Mr J R Lee
42 High Street
Brading, PO36 0DJ
tel: 01983 407560 www.brading.co.uk

**Newchurch Parish History Society**
Bob West
1 West Avenue
Lake
tel: 01983 402600
email: bobanddiwest@cwcom.net

**Sandown and District Historical Association**
Mr J Toogood
16a Cross Street
Sandown, PO36 8BQ
tel: 01983 403075

**Ventnor and District Local History Society**
Mrs F Brown
34 Newport Road
Ventnor
tel: 01983 854057 www.ventnorheritage.org.uk

**Farringford Tennyson Society**
Mrs E Hutchings
Corner Cottage
Hunnyhill
Brighstone
tel: 01983 740363
email: elizabethh@bigwig.net

**National Trust, Newtown Old Town Hall**
Mrs R Noyes
Ken Cottage
Upper Lane
Brighstone, PO30 4AT
tel: 01983 741052

**Cowes Heritage**
John Groves
14, Nodes Road
Northwood
Cowes
tel: 01983 299221

**Cowes Group, Isle of Wight Society**
Mrs Susan Cockram
Flagstaff Antiques
Bath Road
Cowes, PO31 7RH
tel: 01983 200138

**East Cowes Heritage Centre**
8 Clarence Road
East Cowes, PO32 6EP
tel: 01983 280310 www.wight.co.uk

**Newport Group, Isle of Wight Society**
Mr P Gustar
The Bungalow
Heytesbury Farm
Hunnyhill
Newport
tel: 01983 525516

**Parkhurst Prison Heritage Centre**
Mr John Kingsbury
tel: 01983 523855

**Carisbrooke Castle Museum, Friends of**
Mrs Sheila Caws
Hillis Side
Rew Street
Gurnard
tel: 01983 200280

**Island Friends of Royal Osborne**
Mrs D Chillcott
Royal Apartments
Osborne House
East Cowes, PO32 6JY
tel: 01983 200022

**Oglander Roman Trust**
Brading Roman Villa
Morton Old Road
Brading

**Historical Association: Isle of Wight Branch**
Terence Blunden
20 Halberry Lane
Newport, PO30 2ER
tel: 01983 524410

**Isle of Wight Industrial Archaeology Society**
Jill Reilly
34 Madeira Road
Ventnor, PO38 1HW
tel: 01983 853612  www.iwias.org.uk

**Isle of Wight Natural History and Archaeological Society**
Salisbury Gardens
Dudley Road
Ventnor, PO38 1EJ
tel: 01983 855385  www.iwnhas.org

**Isle of Wight Branch of Young Archaeologist's Club**
County Archaeology Service
Archaeology Centre
61 Clatterford Road
Carisbrooke, Newport, PO30 1NZ
e-mail: freespace.virgin.net/iw.history/yac/yac.htm

**Isle of Wight Postcard Collectors Club**
Ron Kemp
18, Manor Crescent
Rookley, PO38 3NS
tel: 07746 174794
Email: ron@ronkemp.co.uk  www.ronkemp.co.uk

**Fire Preservation Society**
Mr K J Kitcher
2 Little Preston Road
Ryde, PO33 1DG
tel 01983 615133

**Historical Vehicle Club, Vectis**
Mr Nigel Offer
10 Paddock Drive
Bembridge , PO35 5TL
tel 01983 872609

**Isle of Wight Riflles Living History Club**
Mr G L Sprack
13 Colenuts Road
Haylands
Ryde
tel: 01983 563156

**Wireless Museum**
Mr D Byrne
52 West Hill Road
Ryde
tel: 01983 567665

**Wolfguard, Dark Ages Society**
Julie Golder
57 Clarence Road
Newport , PO30 1EW
tel: 01983 527677

**World Ship Society, IW Branch**
Mr A Westmore
29 Queens Road
Cowes,
tel: 01983 295550

**Buildings Preservation Trust, IW**
Mr Ian G Smith RIBA
Directorate of Development
Seaclose Offices
Fairlee Road
Newport , PO30 2QS
tel: 01983 823564